Cc

MW01234474

A Collection of Inspirational
Short Stories and Poems
from
Unity North Atlanta Church

Edited by Sara Crawford

Edited by Sara Crawford
www.SaraCrawford.net

Cover design by Lester Herbertson

Photography by Gail Hogue

Printed in the United States of America

First Printing, 2015

ISBN 978-0692450666

Unity North Atlanta Church
4255 Sandy Plains Rd.
Marietta, GA 30066

www.UnityNorth.org

Contents

CONTENTS

CONTENTS

CONTENTS

CONTENTS

Introduction

Since time began, stories have kept alive tradition, history, ancestry, and spiritual practice. Through stories, we transcend boundaries of time and space and create sacred community between storyteller and listener, reader and subject, experience and emotion. This book is a collection of such stories and poems, born of the heart and woven into a tapestry of love that is Unity North Atlanta Church.

Each writer has taken the time to open themselves and share something beautiful and important to them. This is a sacred act. Some stories or poems open the window of our history while others give testimony to the ways God is working in our community today. Some pieces are deeply emotional, others will make you snicker, and still others will cause you to pause and contemplate. No matter the tone, every one of them is important to the Divine idea of UNAC and gives rise to a greater sense of family. I am so grateful for every writer and the glimpse they have offered us into their soul.

Whatever prompted you to pick up this book and give it a look, I thank you as well, and hope that in your reading, a deeper sense of Oneness is born: Oneness with our community, our spiritual tradition, and God.

I offer special thanks to Sara Crawford for her diligent efforts in putting this collection together. Her work as editor, writer, publisher, etc. is so appreciated and a testimony to faith and love in action.

At UNAC, our mission statement is, *"Unity North Atlanta Church is a loving and diverse community inspiring spiritual growth and universal harmony through demonstrations of gratitude, joy, and service."* This collection is a testimony to our mission statement, and I thank each of you for participating in the adventure that is UNAC. Welcome to our hearts. Welcome to our stories. Welcome to our family. Welcome home!

Reverend Richard Burdick

Hope

Brian Perry

Hope. That was literally her name. In the midst of one of the darkest times I had ever known in my life, I walked into Unity North Atlanta Church to listen to Marianne Williamson speak, and the first person to greet me was a woman named Hope. She walked up and hugged me warmly. Right on time.

To my mind, anyone that gets up early on a Sunday, abandoning the promise of a cozy bed and a lazy morning, is seeking something. For me, it was hope. Unity North crossed that off the list before I even found a seat. From then on, UNA has been a profound force of support and encouragement in my world, refusing to allow me to see myself as anything less than I am.

During that first Unity experience, I sat house right, almost hiding. As I mentioned, Marianne Williamson was speaking, and she was/is a bit of a "guru" in my world. I came in knowing no one, freshly arriving from New Orleans on the heels of a divorce. As I sat down, I was in a tremendous place of loss. I'd lost a marriage to a woman I loved. I'd lost virtually every dime that I had. I'd lost the city I loved. My internal story was one of "I'm at loss. I'm at loss. I'm at loss."

And I remember Miss Marianne walked on to the platform (and for me, there was a bit of the sense of Elvis entering the building), and she dove right into her talk with something like this:

"Let me get this clear up front. I'm going to talk a lot about God and faith here. And some of you are thinking, 'I love that whole *Our Deepest Fear* thing I saw you do on Oprah, but I'm not so much about the faith piece.' Let's be very, very, very clear. Every single person on this planet in every second, in every minute, in every hour, of every day has faith. The only question EVER is in what. Is your faith in the disease or the cure? The lonely or the unity? The fear or the love?"

What I took away from that insight is this: when you become intentional about that choice, placing your Faith moment by moment, your world becomes profoundly empowered, your world shifts radically to one of your own perspective, of your own making.

Unity teachings were once framed as "practical Christianity." In other words, the life and parable of Jesus has the greatest value in the extent to which it reminds us of our own capacity to shine the light of love in the world. I've had the honor of speaking and singing from the platform at Unity North, and this community has always managed to see the "Christ-light" in me even when I can't. More importantly, they just will not abide with me trying to turn it down one bit.

Though I'm not in the congregation every week, the congregation is in me, and I am so very grateful. I am more of who I most want to be in the world, living a life of love and abundance regardless of the circumstances of my day-to-day world. I am more of me because I walked through the doors of Unity North Atlanta and into the arms of hope and love.

Listening to the Music Within
Julie Boniger

You never forget the moment you hear the words "you have cancer". It's true what they say – you feel the blood rush from your head, the voices seem farther away, and from that moment on, time is marked as B.C (before cancer) and A.C (after cancer). What I didn't realize in those first moments, however, is what an amazing journey I was about to embark on over the next year, and how crucial my Unity principles would be to my survival.

I was raised Catholic as were both my parents, but from an early age, I had some real concerns about some of the dogma. I could relate to God, the grandfatherly man clad in white robes with a long beard, but I would often think, "I'm just like Jesus. Why are we praying to him?"

Twenty-five years later, my mother called me and said, "I don't believe it, but there is a religion that believes what you have been saying all these years. It's called Unity."

I walked into Unity North in December of 2006. The band was rockin', and people greeted me as if I was their long lost relative. The feeling of love and acceptance was overwhelming. Shortly after the service began, they sang "I am

Divine," and with tears streaming down my face, I thought "I'm home!"

I've always loved to sing and did theatre most of my life, but I was always cast as a dancer. I'd watch the leading ladies stand in the middle of the stage, the spotlight illuminating them as they sang the 11th hour song that poured their heart out on the stage and think, "I would give ANYTHING to experience that." Singing is magical. It takes a concept or feeling, and through the lyrics allows the audience to experience the sentiment on a deeper, more emotional level that uses both sides of your brain. As the singer, it takes you to a place that touches your very soul. The problem was that I had somewhere received the message that I couldn't sing. Maybe it was something that someone said in passing about me being "the dancer", or some self-imposed limiting belief, but I began to develop stage fright.

I participated in choir and did an occasional worship team, and each time, I would panic. People would chide me because I refused to sing into the microphone! In fact, if you put my name into YouTube, you will see a video where Rev. Richard literally reaches over and pushes me toward the mic!

As I began to delve deeper into Unity principles, however, and absorb the unconditional love of the congregation, I began to truly understand that I was a reflection of the divine. Without consciously developing a practice, I began to take "human Julie" out of the equation. My role is to inspire the congregation by connecting us to each other and the Divine Source through song. It's not about me; therefore it's not about any talent I have or don't have.

I'd been asked to do a solo several times and declined, but a good friend told me that if I went inside and connected with Source, I'd be able to discern whether it was fear stopping me or it wasn't the right time. Three years after singing in the choir and small groups, the inner voice said it was time.

Rev. Richard asked me to sing a song to support his talk on dealing with our "core wounds". Unfortunately, nerves actually compromise your ability to sing well. How unfair! I just kept telling myself that this was not about talent but about facing my fear, connecting with the audience, and persevering for something I loved. I hid behind the lyrics, didn't take any vocal chances, and cried at the end, but the most amazing thing happened. As I sang, people stood and sent me energy. The support was palpable and from the applause, you would think I was Barbra Streisand (who by the way has terrible stage fright).

Fast forward to today. If you had told me in 2007 that I would be on staff at Unity North as the Worship and Music Coordinator, singing weekly, leading ensembles and producing Broadway Cabarets, I would have laughed at you. In the recent Broadway Cabaret I produced, I finally had the opportunity to accomplish my own personal goal to sing with abandon. To allow the Source energy to "sing through me" fully and completely. To be that singer that I witnessed from the wings so long ago.

At the end of "Maybe This Time," a song close to my heart, the music stops, and through an epic note, the singer loudly proclaims to the Universe, "This is it!" I went for it, and it was the greatest moment of my performance life. Not because I sang it well but because I did so with abandon.

My journey with stage fright paved the way to allow me to successfully navigate my journey with breast cancer this past year. It's the best thing that ever happened to me. It's a gift that puts into perspective what is important and what isn't, and it allows you to fully understand how loved you truly are. I lived in more joy during my eight months of treatment than in the previous two decades.

One day as I was giggling at my mom's dog leaping through the yard, I thought, "Am I delusional?" My cancer was not caught early. I had five lymph nodes involved and it was highly aggressive. I was told that there is less than a 30% chance I will be here in 5 years and less than a 10% chance I'll be here in 10. How could I be so full of joy?

The answer is fairly simple. I lived almost exclusively in the moment. I was given less than ideal news almost daily, and I had to make decisions that would decide if I lived or died. If I thought about it all at once, I would have gone crazy. We all know the freedom of living in the now, which is truly all we have, but it is difficult to do in the "real world" of work, errands, and retirement planning. Cancer gave me the gift of experiencing that freedom.

I'm back in the world now, and it's difficult. I remind myself daily that I only have now, and my job is to be of service, remember my connection to Source, and experience as much joy and love as I can. And I am not a statistic. Those numbers mean nothing.

I truly owe my life to Unity North. I was given the tools, support, and love I needed to overcome my greatest fear, which prepared me for cancer. My goal is to spend the rest of my life, whether 5 years or 50, inspiring others to be able to break free from self-limitations to express their highest self, whether it be singing, speaking, or climbing Mount Everest. I will also dedicate my life to helping others navigate cancer. Living in service is what truly connects us to each other and Source; it reminds us that we are all indeed One, part of the collective whole. Thank you Unity North for these gifts. I am forever grateful.

I am Whole, I am Complete, I am Enough

Taylor Box

I first came to Unity North back in May of 2014, but I had heard of the Unity Movement about a year earlier. At the time, I was a complete mess: institutionalized in a treatment center in Texas for behavioral and substance addictions. While at this place of refuge, I was safe to explore, for the first time, spirituality without religion. I had grown up staunchly Christian and even feared that I may become possessed by demons during the required weekly yoga and meditation times at the treatment center. However, as I allowed the staff and other clients, who came from many religious backgrounds, to love me simply for being me, my heart began to melt.

A few of the therapists mentioned they were metaphysical Christians, a phrase I had never heard of prior to this time. They emphasized the healing power of love and how God was everywhere, expressing in all things as all things. While here, Reverend Leo Boothe, a former Catholic Priest turned Unity Minister, came and spoke about the difference between spirituality and religion and how all paths lead to the one true God. It was so refreshing and relieving to embrace this message of unity, completeness, and oneness!

I began forgiving myself and others and letting go of the feelings of fear, guilt, shame, and unworthiness that had stalemated my life journey up to this point. I began letting go of the voices that told me I was an addict, someone who was broken. Not enough. As I continued on the path of recovery, I relocated to a religiously affiliated treatment center in Woodstock, Georgia where I graciously and humbly faced my orthodox Christian roots and left them behind. I just knew, despite the love I experienced from the staff and clients there, I no longer fit into the way I used to practice Christianity.

I was no longer looking to be saved by a power greater than myself because I had come to know that I was born good, I was an expression of love, and I was never, ever separate from God in the first place. I loved Jesus but felt uncomfortable worshipping him, believing that he was punished by God so that I did not have to be punished. I began praying about attending a Unity Church.

I will never forget walking into Unity North my first Sunday and feeling an overwhelming sense of peace, love, and acceptance. I truly felt at home for the very first time. I still remember Richard leading silent meditation. I clearly heard the still small voice of Spirit gently and soothingly say, "Be a child and walk with me." Despite all odds, I have been doing so ever since. Jesus did say that we must become like little children to enter the kingdom.

At Unity North, I found the door wide open and welcoming. I have built solid, healthy relationships with people who I can clearly tell love me for who I am, which has helped me to love myself and love others. I have been encouraged to explore more deeply my musical talents and ability to teach others. Getting involved in this spiritual community through A Course in Miracles, choir, Wednesday night meditations, and a young adult group has radically transformed my life. Not only do I no longer see myself as a broken and impoverished individual plagued by addiction, but I am preparing for a life-long journey of preaching and teaching the Good News that Jesus taught. His message was and still is that we have never, ever been separate from our Source, God, the All-Encompassing Good and that nothing is broken or missing in our lives. And so it is as a beautiful song I learned back in treatment says: *I am whole, I am complete, I have everything I need, I am enough.* Thank you, God!

Undefined

Marilyn Boniger

I am a woman.

The Year is 1885.

Men define my worth.

They tell me what I can do;

They tell me, "Don't worry your pretty little head".

Outwardly, I accept;

But somewhere deep inside a voice says,

"You are more than their narrow definition."

A few of my sisters have cried out

      and struggled to become more…

I have seen their tears.

My fear:

If I become more,

I will not fit inside their definition.

It is too narrow.

What will I become?

What are my limits?

I am confused

I need to 'fit'.

I am afraid.

I am a woman.

The year is 1985.

Men define my worth.

They tell me I can do more,

      But they pay me less.

They tell me, "You've come a long way, baby".

Outwardly, I try to reason;

But somewhere deep inside a voice says,

"You must help them to understand."

Many of my sisters are crying out

      And struggling to become what each is meant to be.

I have shared their tears.

My fear:

If I am to grow,

I must leave the protective shell

      That has defined me.

It is too constricting.

I am vulnerable.

I am at risk.

I must try.

I am a woman.

The year is 2085.

My individuality defines my worth.

It tells me what I can do.

God tells me, "I have made you in my image and likeness."

Outwardly I rejoice;

But somewhere deep inside a voice says,

"Because you have known the struggle,

     you must guard the dignity of all people."

All of my sisters

     and brothers

Have helped each other to become

     what each is meant to be.

I have celebrated their success.

My fear:

That jealousy, greed or hunger for power

     will destroy the delicate balance.

The balance that allows all people,

     male and female

To reach their full potential.

We are vigilant

We are happy

We are free.

My Journey to Unity
Diane Glynn

I was raised Catholic. Not the "you must go to Church every Sunday or you will burn in Hell" Catholic, although the nuns wanted me to be that way. Rather we were the Catholics that went to Church just enough to keep the guilt in check. My family leaned more toward the liberal side, but Catholic school was far superior to public education.

My favorite story that explains my mother's relationship with the nuns has to do with my hair. I was a towhead – very light blonde. In fifth grade, Sister Leonardine called me out into the hall. Now, that was scary. However, she didn't yell at me but simply asked what I put in my hair to make it so light. Seriously. I was ten years old and had not a clue what she was talking about.

I answered, "Umm, I think it gets lighter in the sun, Sister."

Sister Leonardine replied, "The sun isn't out this time of year." Really. She did. She had me so confused and frightened that my parents had a hard time consoling me. The next day, my indignant mother gave me a note for Sr. Leonardine that read:

Dear Sr. Leonardine,

Nothing has touched the head of my daughter except the hand of God.

Sincerely,
Mrs. Williams

Yes, that tells you how little the Church frightened my mother.

By the time I reached high school, I was questioning everything. It was around this time that the Church began to lighten up on the rules and I became jaded. *What do you really believe? We are all Children of God but are born into Original Sin? Nuns and priests sign on forever? Mass was the word of God magically expressed through the priests?* And those priests...

We finally broke completely from the Catholic Church when we learned that the priest that married Dan and me was arrested for pedophilia. This man not only married us, he baptized our daughter and had dinner at my house. I was done.

It took many years to release that anger. Never again would I step foot in a church. Never again would I allow a church to dictate how I live my life. Along the way, Dan and I had many conversations about religion and spirituality. We knew that organized religion was too secular but also knew that at the root of all of them, there was love. Unfortunately, most religions were so distorted that love got lost in the "my way or the highway" mentality. So we let it be.

Through friends, we met a man, a Guru, in upstate New York. We visited his ashram many times and brought our daughter there often. We studied the teachings of Yogananda and sang and listened to the Guru speak of peace and love and all things good. Yet, for me, something felt not quite right. Why were these young, very beautiful, women living there and acting as servants in awe of this man? My core has always been my guide, and it was twisting in angst between the teachings and the appearance of something different. Slowly, we began to break away.

Shortly after we moved to Georgia, we learned that our self-proclaimed Guru had committed suicide following an investigation into allegations of sexual molestation of young women who belonged to his ashram. I vowed never again to allow a human to "show me the way". I would, and still do, allow my core to keep my heart in check. My brain, well, it listens to the other two.

During all this time – all the way back to before our daughter was born, Dan's mother had been giving us a subscription to a little monthly publication called *The Daily Word*. It was her way as a devout Catholic, I think, to try and save our souls. Interestingly, our pseudo-Guru also subscribed to *The Daily Word*. What I didn't know until years later that it was a Unity publication and that there were actually churches associated with this little daily devotional.

Fast forward to Georgia. We moved here because of family and cost of living. My parents had passed, and the cost of living in New York was rapidly pushing our limits. Georgia was beautiful year round with no real snow, and we had great family connections. We were fine without a church; we still had spiritual practices. We didn't need anything more… until I saw Unity North Atlanta being built five minutes from my home.

Where did I see that word Unity before? I went home and began searching and, lo and behold, *The Daily Word* popped up. Well, I will admit that I sat there and stared for a few minutes as the pieces began to fall into place. This little book that had made such a difference in our lives was associated with a church that was being built within three miles of my house and, yet, the journey to this place had begun 25 years before.

It took another three to four years before we walked through the doors. In 2006, we were forever changed. We continued to go back week after week. For months, we would go to service and then go to breakfast to talk about it. We were excited, but apprehensive about being sucked in once again. This was different, though. I never got that twisted feeling in my core. Very quickly, we became heavily involved. We became members, we volunteered, we participated in events, we began to tithe, we took classes, we involved our kids, and we began a journey that continues to this day. The reason is simple. The Unity Principles are simple. Above all this, we learned and began to understand the beautiful power of prayer and meditation.

It all stems from love. It sounds so simplistic but we have learned that from love, all else is formed. From love comes kindness, joy, patience, laughter, peace, song and dance. From love, better decisions are made. Life choices become simpler. God/Universe/Spirit/Me/You – it's all the same. And if this is true (and I have come to know it is) then the connection with everything means that everything has beauty and everything has a lesson – even that which is hard to see with my human eye. Even those experiences that once jaded me.

Unity North Atlanta is not a church that can be controlled by any human. It is not a church at all. It is a place of love where spirituality is simply a way of life. It has made me stronger because we simply recognize that through prayer and meditation, if we release our preconceived ideas, God will guide us in the right direction. A new paradigm has been born. This place is here, not because another church is needed for people to go to or someone needs to have a place to showcase their power, but because a place is needed where love lives. This is what you feel when you walk through the doors. It's palpable.

We are making a difference in our own lives and in the lives of the people we come in contact with every single day. Ego does not last here. Ego is made to feel very uncomfortable and either it will take you out the door or it will leave on its own allowing the love to lift you up to a place you never want to leave. As I look back over the past decades, I can now recognize how divinely guided we were (as we all are, yes?). These lessons taught me that what is not in alignment with what is true is not sustainable; they have brought me to where I am now.

It truly is a wonderful way to live. I have been so changed by this journey and the people whose lives I have touched, whose lives have touched me. Whether through Unity, my family or my work, people have honored me with the gratitude they have for the difference we are making. The Unity Principles have brought clarity to the truth I have felt in my core. I no longer practice my spirituality but I *live* it.

Unity North – the Journey does lie within each of us.

When the Student is Ready, the Teacher Will Appear
Kris Anderson

In 1978, I was newly married and living and working in Naperville, Illinois. I was looking for a way to get involved in my community and joined a yoga class to meet new people. I was not familiar with New Thought or Meditation at the time so it came as a surprise to me when, at the end of the *asanas*, the instructor led us in a meditation and guided us to "concentrate on the third eye – that place between the eyebrows." The light I experienced was blinding, and it gave me a headache.

I went up to the instructor and asked her about what I had experienced. She suggested I pick up a book on meditation and learn more about the third eye chakra and the pineal gland. Although there are many explanations on the concept of the third eye, the one I found most interesting is that it is a metaphor for non-dualistic thinking. The first eye is our human eye (sight) and our second eye is our eye of reason (where we make sense of what we see). The third eye operates at a level of awareness of a Christ-like consciousness, where we are in awe of the mystery, the all-ness that connects us with everything.

This third eye observation is where I go when I meditate and wait for answers from the unconscious mind.

When I went to my local bookstore and picked up a beginner's book on meditation, I found a list of people who helped contribute to the book. One name stood out to me: Stephen Stepus. It was the same name of my sister's godfather. I knew that my godparent's last name was "Stenger," but we moved away when I was very young, and I never met them. My parents lost touch with them as the years went by. My sister's godfather was one of my Dad's dearest friends, and they kept in touch over the years.

I called my Dad and asked him if he knew if Stephen Stepus was a religious or spiritual person. My Dad said that Stephen was educated by the Jesuit brothers and wanted to become one of them, but Stephen was a gay man and was rejected by the Catholic Church. After much soul-searching, he turned to New Thought and began counseling gay couples. I called Stephen and we began a correspondence that lasted many years until his death in 2013.

Back in those days, Stephen would record meditations on a tape recorder and send me the tapes; he would send books or recommend books from Unity Village, and he would write me letters sharing his insights and observations. The first metaphysical book he gave me was written by a woman who lived in Kennesaw, Georgia: *Key to Yourself* by Dr. Venice

Bloodworth. Her book was first published in 1952 – the year I was born. I read it and wept. She introduced me to the concept of Universal Mind and Universal Laws and taught me how to use the power of creative thought to create my reality. It was mind-blowing, mind-altering, and life-changing stuff for me.

For the next 20 years, I read every *Daily Word* and *Science of Mind* newsletter and magazine I could get my hands on. And the books... oh the books! My favorite authors were Harriet Emilie Cady, Emmet Fox, and James Dillet Freeman. I would read a principle and deliberately and intentionally incorporate it into my daily life. Life finally made sense. Challenges made sense. Successes made sense. Failure made sense. There was no one or no one *thing* to blame. All was unfolding as it should. I realized that the "more I knew," the "less I knew." And it made perfect sense.

The principles served me well as my husband and I moved frequently with our jobs in the technology industry. In 1996, we moved to Alpharetta Georgia, and in 2001 my sister, who lives in Marietta, told me that a church called Unity was recently built down the street from her home, and she would drive by it occasionally. She said the church marquee would list speakers or topics that she thought I would enjoy.

One Sunday, I decided to make the drive from Alpharetta to check it out even though I was hesitant to go. I had been so happy with my independent studies; I didn't want to have some "organized" church contradict or interpret differently what I felt was spiritual truth. I was so happy that my first visit was one of pure joy. I cried like a baby throughout Carole's thought-provoking message. She spoke my language! I knew I had found my spiritual home. To this day, Unity continues to nourish me. I am so grateful for this spiritual community, its leaders, and its congregants.

It Happened to Me
Sandra Owen

I can barely remember going to bed on Monday night.
I awoke on Tuesday with a sort of knowing that all was not
quite right with me. I could not focus. I knew that I should be
calling my friend, Julie, to see if we would be meeting for lunch
but for some reason, I did not know what to do with my phone
to accomplish this task.

As time passed, I was aware that the day was passing
without any action being taken and that darkness was once
again falling. I remember thinking *maybe I should eat*, but I did
not know how to get this done. I found some bottles of water
and was able to open a bottle and drink some. It was now dark
outside, and I decided to go back to my bed. I was extremely
surprised that it was still unmade.

I crawled into bed and woke up again when it was light
wondering if I would be able to accomplish the appointment
scheduled for the day, but as I saw the light outside wane, I
knew this might not happen.

I vomited what looked like a strange substance, and I
was unable to wash it down the drain which bothered me.
Sometime later, I heard someone knocking at my door, and I
was able to open the door. There stood Julie. I tried to explain

to her what I thought was going on. I heard her say, "I need to call 911" and she tried to get me to sit down. I was insistent about getting her to see the vomit in the sink, feeling that it was important to whatever was happening to me.

Julie came with me to view the contents in the sink. She then got me to finally sit down, and she went outside to call 911. Upon her return inside my apartment, I clearly knew her and spoke succinctly saying "I know you" along with a lot of garbled words, and she gently and lovingly guided me back to the sofa and had me sit down. I felt very safe; my friend was there.

What happened next was somewhat of a blur. Some men in firemen uniforms showed up, and because I felt safe with Julie being there, I did not try to understand what was going on. Suddenly, I was on a gurney being transported to Kennestone Hospital, and someone was asking me a number of questions. At some stage, I became aware that my cousins were also with me at the hospital.

In a wave of consciousness, I was able to communicate to Julie that I did not think she needed to be here as I was suddenly aware that she was undergoing chemotherapy for breast cancer. Her mother, Marilyn, concurred and so Julie left. I sensed a very clear feeling of distress coming from my cousin, Daria, and felt her panic that I might die before her wedding. I felt the strong need to reassure her that I would not die but this communication did not go well as my thoughts and my words were not in sync with each other. I made a mental note to communicate this to her once my speech came back.

After failing to communicate with anyone around me, I felt that I was just an observer and did not even try to participate. Suddenly, I was in a room with two nurses and they seemed to be putting a catheter in me with some difficulty. One of them had an Asian accent, and I could not quite follow what she was saying but felt her anxiety as she requested the other nurse to assist her in completing the task. Eventually, it was done, and I was taken to another room.

Sometime later, when I came to, my cousin's finance, Bianca, was with me and after unsuccessfully trying to communicate with her, I began to feel my right shoulder and arms shake in an alarming way. It felt as if someone or something was trying to tear my right arm from my body with the speed of a train that has lost control. This was the first time since the stroke that I experienced real fear.

Bianca got the nurses to the room. They calmed me down and the movement stopped. Apparently, I had a seizure. In my mind, a few minutes had passed and another attack rocked my right shoulder and arm again. The nurses were there almost immediately and told me to ride it through as this was not going to be more than a few seconds. I trusted her and in my head it lasted about five seconds.

When I came to again, I saw Bianca and this time when I spoke to her, I heard myself speak clearly if not slowly. Bianca got on her phone and told my cousins that I was speaking again. Immediately, my thoughts went to a prayer of thanksgiving and immediately I felt the warmest glow of light and love surround and fill me as I heard from a place deep within me that I would be fine, no matter which side I woke up on, and the word "fear" lost its power over me in that moment. All was well.

After discovering that Kennestone Hospital did not take my insurance, I was transported to Northside Hospital but not before the very kind nurses at Kennestone helped me shower, which was very invigorating. Over the next few days, a number of friends, relatives, and members of Unity North Atlanta Church as well as One World Church showered me with healing thoughts and kindness. Some of my friends and family called me, others visited and sat with me in the hospital while others even brought me mango slices. Soon Northside Hospital discharged me and my friend, Corinna, took me to her home where I spent the next six weeks recuperating with her family.

The power of God's will is strong and mysterious and connects us all with its infinite source of love. With the determination, caring, and steadfastness of Dawn Gowing, Julie Boniger, and Corinna Jones, I am blessed to have been given a second chance at life and to be surrounded with such a wonderful community of friends and family. I now wake up each and every day giving thanks to the grace of God. And so it is and so it shall be, Amen.

Unity North, These are my People!
Dawn Morris

My spiritual beliefs were never mainstream.

A divorced family,

one weekend Baptist,

the other Methodist.

How could God love either any less?

But into Unity North I walked...

Did I hear this right?

Many Paths, One God!

Could this be?

Can they actually think like me?

Oh yes, these are my People.

The Bible is a guide?

Don't take it literally?

Could this be true?

For so long, I thought I was one of few.

Yes, yes, these are my People.

Higher Consciousness,

Positivity,

Divine Mind,

Meditation,

Enlightenment,

This I've known to be true.

Yes, yes, yes, Unity North, You are my People!!

An Ancient Life Saver

Claudia Bell

I have been practicing the Ho'oponopono prayer and it has a profound impact on my life. It is an ancient Hawaiian prayer for healing sent to the Divine based on the concept that everything in our world is connected. The Hawaiians believe that nature including humans, animals, plants, and even minerals are One. We are supposed to live together in harmony and peace, respecting all things present. It is a simple yet powerful prayer, and the more often we say it, the more we can "clean" our world from toxic influences and heal it.

I am sorry;

Please, forgive me;

Thank you;

I love you.

On Good Friday, I released and let go of all expectations and attachment to my old group of friends. Something happened in the beginning of the year that caused a huge shift for me. After wading through what I consider now a "swamp of hell," I realized that I could no longer go on with the way things were. My friend introduced me to Ho'oponopono, and I have been praying for myself and the whole world daily since then. I am feeling increasingly at peace and liberated. I feel more in charge of my life and have finally managed to stop feeling like a victim. Hallelujah!

Having been a survivor all my life, these last winter months felt not only horrifying, but I also didn't feel like myself. I felt completely lost, hopeless, helpless, and in constant pain in an intensity I had never felt before. I've always found a way to pull myself back together and to move on from hardship. This time was different.

The more time passes, the more I begin to grasp the possible lessons for me. I truly believe that everything happens for a reason. Not everything happens *intentionally*; that is why we wonder why things happen to us. But instead of asking God why these things happen to us and why we have to live through such difficulties, we need to learn to trust and know that in time we will understand. If we take the blame off other people and replace anger and hatred with love and forgiveness, we are able to move on in peace. If we believe that everything is part of a Divine plan, we can let go of the need to figure out why *right now* because we will learn in time when we are ready. The more time we spend in silence listening to God, the sooner we will find the answers and true peace.

Wayne Dyer says, "Be passionate about your life and live it to the fullest and you will have everything you need and more. The key is to let go of the outcome!" It took me a very long time to understand what he meant by "letting go of the outcome." I have finally gotten it! When I think back on all the despair I felt this winter, I feel like I wasted precious time and energy. I was so lost and so disconnected from myself that I was incapable of seeing what I needed to do. God was waiting for me to connect with him, but I didn't know what I was supposed to do. I felt isolated, abandoned, and hurt.

It was in these many hours alone (even while I hated every minute of it rather than seeing the opportunity for growth) that I learned about myself. I learned that I had lost touch with my inner self. I had been spending too much time giving to others and doing many meaningless things in the physical world. I had not been feeding my soul, and I had not been in touch with my God. I had lost my sense of self-love, and my intuitive gift was buried under unimportant worldly thoughts and concepts.

Only when we spend time in silence and turn inward for guidance will we become more at peace with ourselves. I knew that! I had been living with those ideas and principles for many years. What had happened to me to not be able to see that? I learned a long time ago that I only find out what I need to be passionate about and what my true purpose is when I listen to God. Why could I not see that anymore?

We get so involved in human drama that we can't see what is really important for our spiritual growth. Our problems and concerns in the physical world can seem so big and overwhelming, yet they really aren't if we look at them as growth opportunities and lessons. In the heat of the moment, hardships can feel impossible to overcome. Yet, we survive. We continue living. It is up to us to grow and learn from those experiences. We can become bitter or fearful of new relationships or close ourselves off from the world. Those are completely justifiable and normal reactions if we believe that we are alone and have to battle life's difficult times by ourselves.

If we let go of the outcome or, in other words, if we decide not to worry about how things will end up, we can free our soul from the pain. If we believe that "all will be good and that in time we will know and understand," if we trust in God and give up our need to control the situation (the idea that we have control is just an illusion anyway), we can go on in peace. We can open to intuition and spiritual lessons instead of desperately hanging on to the feelings of betrayal, injustice, and abandonment. Those feelings are toxic and any thought about them keeps us from making progress in the direction of love and peace. If I believe that we are all One and that we are connected, I can make a difference when I pray for everyone and especially for those with whom I have experienced problems in my physical life. By sending love, forgiveness, and gratitude to them and by asking them to forgive me as often as

I can in a day, I am reducing those toxic feelings in my mind one prayer at a time.

We are all connected; our souls are all part of One.

Let It Set You Free

Sara Crawford

There is nothing wrong
with pausing to admit
you could do with some help
now and then–whether it's from
the leaves buzzing within the trees
or the infinite stars, reminding us
what the past looked like.

Life will put you where you are supposed to be.
Inhale, exhale. Let it set you free.

There's No Place like Home
Lorelei Robbins

When I walked into Unity North Atlanta Church in 1992, which at that time was in a shopping center in Marietta, I felt that I finally found my home. I felt that I fit in and belonged in all my "weirdness". This church was nothing like what I was used to growing up with a mom who was Catholic and a father who was Jewish. I went to Jewish Sunday school until I was eight when I was then baptized in the Catholic Church. Can we say confused? I was used to dogma having spent my high school years in two different Catholic boarding schools in the German and French parts of Switzerland.

When I first read the part of the Unity message that we create our reality through what we think, feel, and believe, I was more than intrigued. This was a totally foreign concept to me. How could it possibly be true that I was doomed trying to make up for sins I didn't even know I committed? Unity North has been the one place where I have always felt understood and seen. It has always felt safe to be me...all of me. For someone who grew up feeling like she never fit in, it has always amazed me that I would walk down such an unconventional path as an astrologer, which just brought up more "opportunities" to feel like I didn't fit in. And it's not that everyone at Unity embraces astrology, far from it; but those who are attracted to Unity are drawn here because freedom of self-expression is encouraged, fostered, and nurtured.

I have watched so many of my friends and fellow Unity enthusiasts blossom and emerge into extraordinary versions of themselves. One of the things that continues to jazz and juice me at Unity is that I feel consistently celebrated and championed by my Unity family to live, express, and be the individualized expression of God that I am. And I have the honor and privilege of showing up in their lives in the same way.

I never really felt "at home in my own skin" until I became a part of the Unity North family. Having the secure emotional foundation I have created and experienced at Unity North has allowed me to step out and be more authentic with greater courage, commitment, and conviction. The feeling of belonging, being at home, and being a contributing member to my spiritual family is one of my greatest passions.

"Walk on, walk on with hope in your heart, and you'll never walk alone…" (*Carousel*). That song accompanied me on my journey as a young child growing up in an upper middle class neighborhood in Manhasset, Long Island. I wandered around alone during the summers waiting for school to start because I had no friends. I was convinced that my parents were the only divorced couple, that we were the only "broken family" in the neighborhood. Whether this was true or not, who knows, but it sure did fit my journey of feeling abandoned, not belonging, and not fitting in. And even though I felt lonely and disenfranchised, deep down I believed that if I wished hard enough, my dreams would come true. Little did I know that was the beginning of my creating the role I would play now in my life as a Dream Accelerator for others.

As a child, I never wanted to leave my room. I felt safe, protected, and cocooned there, while the thought of venturing out filled me with terror. And yet at the same time, one of my fondest memories as a young child was being on the radio with my dad, and creating his show, *Robbin's Nest*, from the den in our home. I was actually the youngest disk jockey in the country at four years of age. Had I been aware of my soul's map (astrological chart), I would have known that once I would feel comfortable and safe, the childlike/playful/showman side of me would emerge, and I could easily establish rapport and engage an audience.

I think back to those days and how much "little Lore" would have benefitted if she had known that her painful shyness, difficulty fitting in, and her need to be in her "sanctuary" were co-created by God and her soul before she was born. As far back as I can remember, all I wanted was to feel that I belonged, but instead I felt that I never fit in. I kept looking to others to define me and tell me who I was. I looked especially to my romantic relationships and jobs to find myself.

In the search to find myself, I married five times from 1970 to 2009. As I write this, it's even hard for me to believe that because each time I married, I was certain that it would last forever and I would at last feel safe.

Even though I've been self-employed since 1981 when I started my personnel consulting business, and then my astrological business, Thank Your Lucky Stars, in 1987, I spent most of my life trying to jump on someone else's bandwagon hoping to get their approval and validation of my worth and my value.

The road to living an authentic life takes courage, commitment, and the willingness to be true to your own, unique path. It can be hard to stay the course and not give up, to consciously choose moment by moment to believe in who you are and what you came here to share with the planet.

The thought that I would "die with my music still inside me" has terrified me and kept me up at night. Once I became aware that the fear was actually motivating me more than the joy of "singing my song," I freed myself from my self-made prison and was able to experience the magic of my own spirit.

Daring to dream has been taking the risk over and over to sing my song no matter what. As Rumi said, "I want to sing like the birds sing, not worrying about who hears or what they think." We have all come to the planet with unique gifts and talents, and when we express them, our heart jumps for joy and our soul rejoices. Unity North continues to be a place where I am nurtured, championed, and celebrated to be all of me.

My Heart is Open
Michael March

When first entering the doors of Unity Church, my inner spirit was revitalized and reborn. Recognizing the unique opportunity, I gave thanks for finally being led to a house of worship that would not only accept me, baggage and all, but be my beacon of light shining brightly through the darkness. Searching, but never quite finding the key to unlock my dreams and melt away my fears for most of my life, I marveled at the miracle I found awaiting me within these walls.

In 1968, as a confused young war veteran, I found an unappreciative and insensitive society. It seemed everyone had lost sight of Godliness and cared only for personal gain, grabbing for a piece of the proverbial pie and discarding their humanity to bow down and worship the "golden idol."

I always believed that people came first, and love of mankind should be nurtured and cherished. Being chastised by my parents for my beliefs, I was sent off to consult a professional counselor who would help me recognize the truth and discard my unrealistic approach to life.

Born of Jewish heritage, I never understood why, in America, I needed to worship in an antiquated fashion and pray in a language from another place and a far distant time. So I searched for an avenue to renew my faith, and I thought I had found it. Dipped into a pool of clear cool water, I was baptized and agreed to accept Jesus Christ as my Lord and savior. It was closer to my personal religious beliefs, but not exactly. I participated in services at the Pentecostal church for a few years, but with a pervading feeling of my being disingenuous, I came to the conclusion that I couldn't, in good conscience, continue to attend.

Then I met Marie and a new lease on life was presented to me. Not only did we connect on an intellectual level but on the spiritual plane as well. Her insightfulness and simple explanations were more statement of facts than opinions.

"Michael, you must come with me to church," she suggested one Saturday morning as we sat sipping coffee at Panera. "You'll love Unity Church," she continued. "It's a 'hippy' church; people are real and loving. I think you'll find it right up your alley."

Those few words were my first introduction to our church and how it all began for me. I couldn't wait to attend my first Sunday service the very next day, and I have not been sorry, only thankful. I have found peace of mind and abundant joy abounds within, wanting to be shared. Not only has it opened my heart and mind to the Unity community but it prompted a rekindling of the partially spent coals, extinguished by years of adherence to a conformist philosophy and turning of a blind eye to what was always before me---the passageway to truth and understanding.

Now I feel those similar optimistic emotions as I did when I was an idealistic twenty-one year old. Those internal feelings of prevailing goodness and love have blossomed once again, and I can't wait to see how each new day unfolds. Knowing that we are all part of the universal fabric of humankind, being of one soul, our hands reach out to welcome all people and share the gift that we have all found.

How Unity Has Changed Me
Michele Strother

"He who is standing, beware he does not fall." This was a favorite scripture quoted by my devoutly religious parents. The message, as interpreted by my seven-year-old mind meant: *Look out. If something good happens and I feel happy about it, something bad will happen.* This became a firm truth wired into me. To be joyful at my own good luck or happy about an accomplishment was to invite disaster. It was best to be wary, prepared for any possible negative eventuality.

So it was, with a near lifetime of this type of thinking, that I entered Unity. Here I was introduced to the concept that positive thinking leads to positive vibrations which lead to more positive, happy experiences. By contrast, negative thinking leads to negative energy which leads to negative experiences. Like attracts like. How bizarre was that? Could it even be true? Had my family and I been wrong about something so basic? Perhaps I should find out.

So, my experiments began. I became consciously glad for my organs and body parts that were doing their job and keeping me healthy. Nothing bad happened. I basked in the glory of a holiday dinner I hosted which went well. Nothing bad happened. In fact, it felt rather nice. It was such a relief not to feel the need to be so guarded. But, oh how difficult to change such an ingrained pattern of thought, especially when dealing with the little occurrences of everyday life.

It was just after Christmas and our six-year-old clothes dryer broke down. My thoughts were on autopilot, and I admit, the old wheels were starting to turn in the wrong direction. It began: *Great. Right after the expense of the holidays. And how old is this dryer, only six years old? I guess I should have expected this. Why does this always* . . . . You get where I was going. Down the whiny, negativity path. But then I realized, all I was doing was lowering my vibration and attracting more negativity towards me. Plus, it didn't feel good. So, I stopped myself midsentence and started over. *After all,* I said to myself, *we generate a lot of laundry in our house. The dryer goes from morning to night nearly seven days a week. It's worked pretty hard for a while.*

My husband unhooked the unwieldy machine, and he and my son hoisted it into the back of our small truck. It was a gray and rainy day and we hoped we could get the new dryer home without it getting drenched. We pulled into Lowes and discovered that most of their dryers were out of stock and that you couldn't just drop off your old dryer there anymore. They could arrange for someone to take it from your house and install the new one free of charge, but you could not drop it off. We found the same situation again at the next store.

Before we continued to look, we decided we had to get rid of the old dryer. It was going to cost approximately forty dollars to drop it off at a dump, which my husband insisted he knew the approximate location of. Somehow, though, we kept going down roads that did not lead us to the dump. And, here's where it got tempting. My old thought process would have been: *Why in the world did we disconnect the old dryer and haul it into the truck without first checking to see if we could drop it off at the store? Now we're stuck unless we want to go home and haul it back out of the truck. If that's not bad enough, we're going all over creation looking for a place to get rid of the thing because my husband thinks he knows where it is, a man who never asks for directions* etc. etc. etc.

I then would have verbalized what I was thinking, and you can guess what would have happened. That's right, a squabble, bad feelings and possibly a ruined afternoon. But, I actually remembered to take charge of my thoughts. Instead I said to myself, *I don't get to have much alone time with my husband. I'll just enjoy the drive and be on the lookout as the right and perfect outcome will happen.* And then, and this is the good part, I actually *felt* like this was true.

To make a long story short, within minutes, we found a place that paid to receive old appliances. They actually gave us money to take our old dryer because they wanted the scrap metal. So instead of losing money, we actually gained some. Then, we had a wonderful dinner out and found an excellent dryer in stock at a good price. What could have been a miserable outing turned into a success. Our thoughts truly create our reality.

Practicing the Principles

Suzie Burdick

Over the last several years, I have worked with middle school kids here at Unity North Atlanta. I have assured them that if they learn three things while participating in Uniteens, it will fortify them for any challenge they may encounter on their life path. First, "Thank you, God" is a complete prayer! Second, instead of naming a situation "good" or "bad," say, "that's interesting!" Third, understand the Five Unity Principles, particularly Principle #3, which says, "I create my experiences by what I choose to think, feel, and believe."

Here are a couple of examples of times when using these ideas helped me to manifest experiences that transcended what seemed possible.

For almost 30 years, my career had been nurturing children in the foster care system. We had nine or ten children living with us in our home for all these years, and I loved the chances I had to help them grow and blossom. When we left California in 1993 for a new adventure in Portland, Oregon, I knew that I still wanted to work with kids, just not 24 hours a day.

I started visioning what that would look like, and I came up with a very specific idea of what I wanted. I wanted to be a nanny to a family with one three-year-old little girl who would love tea parties. I didn't want to have to be at a job early in the morning or stay late in the evening. I wanted $1000 a month, and I wanted the employer to do my withholding taxes.

I applied for a job with an outstanding nanny agency in Portland. They honestly laughed out loud when I told them what I was looking for. They said it would be impossible to find a job like that. They explained that most families looking for a nanny had more than one child, all families they worked with would require me to be at their home very early, and $1000 was out of the question unless it was for a very large family. My interviewer laughed again about withholding taxes and said it was never done.

Although that sounded discouraging, I believed that with God, all things were possible and held in mind that the job I was seeking was also seeking me (Principle #3).

The agency sent me out on several interviews and gave me temporary jobs. None of the jobs fit the description of my ideal job, but I continued to believe in my vision.

Three weeks after signing with the agency, I traveled a long distance for an interview with a family who had one child and another on the way. They would need me from 6:00 am until 6:00 pm. I came home very discouraged and started to cry.

When Richard asked me what was wrong, I said, "They didn't offer me the job!"

He looked at me surprised. "Was that the job you wanted?"

I looked at him with chagrin and admitted, "No, I would have hated that job!"

The next day, I was assigned a temporary job with a family whose nanny had suddenly quit. The family had one three-year-old girl, and after three days, they wanted to interview me for a permanent job. They loved what I had done so far and said I was their "Mary Poppins"! They asked how much money I wanted to make, and I told them $1000. They told me my hours would be 11:00 to 6:00, only four days a week. Here was the job I had envisioned. I had kept the Faith and hadn't settled for something "less than".

After accepting the job, as I walked to the door, the husband said, "By the way, would you like us to do your withholding taxes?"

Thank you, God!

When we moved to Georgia in 2006, we were excited to see how much house we could get for our money and bought a large traditional home. Four years later, realizing we didn't need so much house or upkeep, we yearned to downsize, but the recession had hit hard and real estate values had gone down. It was not a good time to sell a home. We believe that God is Active in all things (Unity Principle #1) and knew that if we kept affirming our intention to find a home better suited for us, then recession didn't make a difference.

Months later, a friend from church called and in the conversation said she wanted to buy our house. She had been to a party at our home the previous year and had fallen in love with it. She wanted to relocate to our school district, and we were in just the right spot, close to all three schools her children would be attending.

I laughed, thinking she was doing some wishful thinking and then changed the subject. After I got off the phone, I started to wonder if she was serious, and I called back to ask if she really wanted to buy our house. So many times we expect things to happen in a certain way and miss the opportunities that present themselves in less conventional ways.

She confirmed that she really did want to buy our home! Because there was no real estate commission, we were able to sell at a price that was agreeable to all. Who could have imagined this scenario?

Now our job was to find the house that was to be our new home. We had parameters. It needed to be close to church, close to our family, a certain price point, etc. We looked at house after house and even made bids on a couple, but none made our hearts sing. We affirmed, "The house we are seeking is seeking us!" (Principles #3 and #4). We knew our right and perfect home was out there, but we felt pretty discouraged the day our realtor told us she had shown us every house on the market that fell into our price range. There was nothing more to see. We returned to center and again affirmed that the house that was ours was waiting for us.

That same afternoon, the realtor called us and said something interesting had happened. A lady had dropped by the realtor's office to see what the possibility might be of listing her house in a couple of weeks after she did some work on it. She wanted to move to a condo but didn't know if she could sell her house when real estate was at the bottom. As this woman described her home, our realtor said she had clients whom she thought would be very interested and asked if she could show it to us.

We knew instantly this was our home. Our hearts were definitely singing! The seller was overwhelmed that a visit to the realtor would bring her an instant sale. She was able to move within three weeks and didn't have to do any repair work or freshening to the house as we were going to do some upgrades.

Three families were blessed as we practiced living the Truth. We create our experiences by what we say, feel, believe and practice. We choose to keep our eyes open and look for the good. We believe, even when it looks impossible!

Home is more than a building and a piece of land. It is where we go to center ourselves, to feel sheltered, a sanctuary for our souls. God within us leads us to our spiritual "home" when we listen to the small voice. We co-create that special place when we partner with Spirit and Belief.

These are only two of many examples of how these Principles have worked for us and helped us to create a life of adventure, of "interesting" moments, and of blessings for ourselves and so many more!

Thank you God!

U HAIKU

Deanna Fleenor

Unity North Church

Helped me recognize my worth;

God and I are one!

Standing in my Power
David Smith

We shook hands, and I watched him drive away. This was not how I had expected the day to go. I might have expected police, guns, yelling, threats, and lies, but not a handshake.

The only reason this day was different than the last month was because I was able to use the principles I learned while attending Unity North Atlanta Church and for the first time in years, I was able to stand with zero fear and claim my power. I claimed that love is more powerful than hate and truth is more powerful than lies. I was able to stand knowing that what I focused on would be my reality and that I was the master of my thoughts.

It was September, and I was living in a house with three other people. Like many people these days, in order to make ends meet, I had boarders living in my home. Unfortunately, this would be the last month that I was on time with rent.

I go to church at Unity North Atlanta, a new thought church based on the teaching of Myrtle and Charles Fillmore. They taught that thoughts are things, and we create our reality based on what we think. I really resonated with this philosophy and have been attending UNA for about 10 years. In that time,

I've watched my children grow up, lived through separation and divorce, and had many other experiences, both challenging and rewarding. Through it all, though, I have always known that things would be okay. I've used these lessons to shape my life and I am living proof that the Unity Principles can change lives for the better.

September came and went, and when October arrived, one of my boarders planned to move to Miami for school. No problem, I thought. I had two more boarders that were ready to move in: Adrian and Geoff, two brothers. At the end of the month, I had another responsible boarder move out so I got another to replace him: Brian.

When November came, all three of them were late with rent. It turns out Brian and Adrian both were fired from their jobs. I sat them down and talked to them, explaining that I knew what it was like to be down and to have money troubles. I think everyone deserves a break, and I sent these young men the love that I would like to have. I began to suspect there were many lies, but I still trusted that things would work out.

In mid-December, after they still hadn't paid rent, I sat them down and told them they would have to find another place to live. They swore to me that they would have rent in a few days; they were all going to borrow money from their parents. Adrian and Geoff had previously told me that their father was a state senator. When I did some research, though, I began to see their lies unraveling as I discovered this wasn't true. I was firm, standing in my power, and I told them they had to leave.

One day, after Adrian had disappeared for a week without a trace, he showed up to claim his belongings. He threatened me with violence, took his stuff, and left. It was almost Christmas, and I knew I had a choice: force the issue and have them out before Christmas or let them stay for the holidays. They still promised me they would have rent. I used the last of my savings to pay the rent they owed, and no money came forth from them. I made the decision to stand in my power and insist they leave.

On Friday, I let them know they must be out by Tuesday at noon. They threatened me, called me names, and there were more lies, but when Tuesday came, I stood in my power. *Today is the day these people must leave.*

I realized that I was going to be out about $1000, but still I stood in my power even when the lies, name calling, and threats kept coming. How could I stay calm and in control when my world was coming down around me? My solution was to turn to the Unity Principles. I visualized what I actually wanted to happen. I made peace with the fact that I may never see the money they owed me. I let go of the anger that came and focused instead on finding a peaceful resolution to the problem.

They finally did leave, telling me they would be back Saturday to collect their stuff, but not without threatening to get violent and/or call the police. I was a little nervous. Saturday and Sunday came and went, though, and no one showed up. On Monday, I cleaned up their rooms and placed their belongings out near the street per eviction procedures. When I texted them to let them know, there were more threats, but still I stood in my power. I repeated that all I wanted was to have them out and have their things out so we could all move on.

When Brian and Adrian came by to get their stuff, they claimed they were missing a dresser and their beds and would be back in the morning with the police to collect them. I hauled these things to the street and told them to come get them, but they refused and offered me more threats.

I called the police and had them come to my house for advice. They called it a "domestic standby" and explained that they did this all the time. When I covered up their stuff to protect it from the weather, the police officer told me I was going above and beyond what he has seen others do. He explained that once the stuff is near the street, it's basically free for anyone to take. I put signs on the tarps so that things would be left alone. I affirmed that all would be resolved tomorrow. There were more threats from Adrian, but I noticed Brian staying calm and I sensed something was changing with him.

The next day, Brian let me know that he was the only one who would be coming to collect things; Adrian was supposed to help, but he claimed to be sick. All of the remaining items belonged to Adrian and Geoff, but Brian was coming to retrieve them. I offered to help him move some of the bulkier things, and when he arrived, we simply shook hands. We loaded up the stuff and had a good talk about how he was starting to realize what kind of people Adrian and Geoff were. We had a few laughs like friends and shook hands once again. He got in his SUV, and I watched him drive off.

As I stood in my yard, I gave gratitude. Things worked out for the best. The situation was finally resolved peacefully, and I was free to move on. The Unity principles helped me to make this happen. I stood in love, and I stood in my power. And all was well.

Finding Where I Belong
Elizabeth Lockley

In 2009, I moved to Georgia from sunny southern
California, where I would attend my "family reunions" as I
called them at Unity by the Sea, then lead by Reverend Jack
Bomar. Raised Catholic, I now always cringe at the word
"church" so I never saw Unity as such.

Moving to Georgia was quite the change, especially as I
"landed" in Conyers, Georgia and felt like I had moved back to
the early 80's. Finally after three years in Conyers, my husband
and I made the move to Marietta (*ahhhhhhhhh much better!*) and a
special bonus was that I now was very close to another Unity.

At first it was quite the shock coming from a small
place in Santa Monica to this magnificent building that Unity
North Atlanta calls home. Amazingly enough, the size did not
affect that feeling of closeness and family. What always
attracted me to Unity was how welcoming they were to all,
especially my gay friends. It has always been a very important
piece for me that everyone is loved and free of judgment no
matter who they love. To see on one of my first visits that even
one of the ministers was gay—the wonderfully refreshing and
authentic Jeanie Ward—and that everyone was perfectly okay
with it made me smile.

Unity makes no one "convert" to anything. We learn about every other tradition out there and embrace it all. Another beautiful thing is that everyone feels comfortable and doesn't stress about "fitting in". Come as you are! Unity North truly is a loving family of many that makes everyone feel at home. When I had to miss a few Sundays, people noticed! They immediately checked up to make sure I was okay or to see if they could be of assistance.

In my search for a warm spiritual home that resonates with my beliefs I found Unity North Atlanta, and the friends I have made there will be in my heart forever.

Color-Blind Soul

Marilyn Boniger

I was born into a world of black and white. Along the way I have learned many facts. In my need to be safe, and good and liked, I turned these facts into truths without questioning if they were truly facts. I was "religiously" taught not to question.

Throughout my childhood and early adulthood, I clung to this color-blind view of the world. I judged people, governments, religions, places and things, even words, to be good or bad, black and white. I grew up in a religion that reinforced these beliefs with the teaching that if there was a truth for me to embrace, it would be revealed to me, not by God, but by the church hierarchy. I was discouraged not only from seeking my own truth, but I was also forbidden to become exposed in any way to other religious ideas and values. Spiritually, I felt as if I was in a vast, barren, beige desert. I tried to fill my spiritual life by doing the work of the church. I chaired committees, became a Lector, Eucharistic Minister, and I even taught religious education to children. Still, I wandered in this spiritual desert becoming thirstier and more lost until I found an oasis called Unity.

The religion of my youth had kept me spiritually immature and caused a kind of spiritual color-blindness. My thirst was not for more facts or even more truths, but for the freedom, without fear of punishment or guilt, to search for my own truths. Unity has given me that freedom.

My first time in a Unity Church was in Pennsylvania. One cold, snowy morning, I drove 20 miles to a small, Unity church. It was definitely a "divine appointment" because by the time the service ended I knew I had "come home". Slowly, my beige desert began to take on color, and truths, MY truths began to take shape.

When I moved to Georgia and began to attend Unity North, I found that my desert had become a lush, colorful garden. Truths are revealed to me on a regular basis through music, classes, talks, special events and the love and support of the people of Unity. I am no longer willing to judge anything as good or bad because through the practical Christianity of Unity, I have discovered that it is all good!

I have also discovered that fact is a concrete reality, something that comes to you through your senses. Facts are the same for everyone. Truth, however, is personal and not absolute, rather it is a belief relative to your experience and not static but constantly changing. Truth is the result of your experiences and how you choose to react to them shapes your values. Attitude is the expression of the truths you hold.

I think of truth as the image you see in a kaleidoscope. The kaleidoscope itself, the mirrors, the particular pieces, their size, shape and color; these are the facts. But truth is the image you perceive, one of beauty and blending of colors. You can hand your kaleidoscope of facts to any number of people and no two will see it the same. Each will turn it and interpret the truth of its beauty for himself.

Facts are constant; truth is relative. Facts are the sunshine and the rain; truth is the rainbow.

Through Unity, I have found that searching for truth is a lifelong quest. Growth requires change and adjustment, often causing pain and discomfort. In order for my truths to mature, I need to listen to others with an open mind, setting aside my truths to hear what could be true for someone else. At this point in my quest, I am not only searching for new truths but to deepen my understanding of the truths I hold.

Schopenhauer says, "The discovery of truth is prevented more effectively, not by the false appearance things present which mislead into error, not directly by weakness of the reasoning powers, but by preconceived opinion, by prejudice."

Along the road I have happily discovered this truth: If facts are black and white, truth is Technicolor.

Web of Wonder
Michael Burke

I heard the wind whistle

Through the webs of wonder

Woven by the spirits of serenity

For just that purpose

To bring outer sound

To inner silence

To capture the breath

Of The Beloved

In Sacred reverberation

And release the blessing

Of the Grace within

I saw crystals dancing

On these strings of infinite patterns

Glistening in the vibration of Love

Pulsing with perfection

Singing with the Saints

Aligned with Angels

Whose tears of joy they represent

By sprinkling free from captured essence

To splash upon Disciples

As they become Apostles

Rooted in the earth

Yet blossoming in Heaven

Captured in their time

Yet beyond that constraint

A vision of the future

Is a look into the past

For where we are going

Is where we came from

And woven in that

Web of wonder

Is All of Us

Before we were

Any of us.

Unity North Atlanta: My Church Family

Rose Anita Renner

I found Unity North by accident.
It was a different church than I thought.
New Beginnings aft' service, I was sent.
Realized I'd found the family, I'd sought.

I was home. I could be me and be free.
For years I'd searched to be free and belong.
There are many paths to One God, you see.
Together we are one and sing our song.

I see more people here living Christ's way,
than in any church I've ever been in.
Five principles for life is all we say.
Positive thoughts are the way that we win.

Come join our family. Just check us out.
The love you will feel is real; there's no doubt.

Brookana

Angie Icard

2006 was an extremely challenging year for myself and Matt. We had severe financial issues, Matt had family issues, and I suffered an extremely painful spinal injury and later in the year spent nearly a month in the hospital with a life threatening issue. After we survived the year from HELL, we were determined to make a new beginning in 2007. We had nowhere to go but up! To accomplish our goal, we attended Unity North Atlanta Church every time they opened the doors.

One class we were in had us each make a vision board. We completed them on Friday April 6, 2007 in time for church on Sunday. We hung them above our bed on the ceiling. We had little girls on them, and each night we would say things like "Won't it be so much fun when our daughter finally gets here!" And, "I can't wait to hold her when she finally arrives." We decided on a name and just focused on the gratitude we felt in preparation for her arrival. I'm not sure I totally "believed" a baby would be delivered on our doorstep.

We were always open to however God wanted to grow our family. Matt and I knew we wanted to be parents together. We spent many hours talking about rules and love and schools and homework and dating, everything that goes into raising a

70

child. Through all this, we concentrated on the gratitude and anticipation of our daughter joining our family.

Fast forward to January of 2008. I was in my lab at work, and my friend (who we now refer to as the stork) came to me and said, "There is a baby girl at Grady. Her birth mom is in jail and she needs a home. Don't you and Matt want a baby girl?"

I answered, "Yes, we do. I need to call Matt." I called him, and he wanted to know if we could bring her home tonight. I said that I didn't have any details but I would find out. I found out that she was 3 months premature and born to a drug addicted mother who had been incarcerated for only 7 days. Her health and survival was unstable at this point. The doctors were not sure what lasting effects she would suffer due to the lack of prenatal care and being exposed to the many drugs during gestation. The birth mother was feeling extreme heartburn and when the baby's heartrate was checked as part of the exam, it was found to be so low that the doctors thought she was in imminent danger and did an emergency C-section to get her out. Once she was out, she was stable.

We finally got guardianship and were able to meet her for the first time. On the way to see her for the first time, Matt and I wondered how we would know she was really our daughter. How would we know she was ours and not really someone else's kid? I told him I knew there would be a sign.

We could not believe how beautiful she was, especially for such a premature baby. She actually smiled for us as soon as she saw us and didn't stop the whole time we visited her apart from when she fell asleep. On the second day we visited her, I asked what day her actual birthday was. Because of all the HIPPA laws, and also since we did not know her birth family, we had little knowledge on her prior to the guardianship. The nurse checked her record and told us January 6th.

On Friday, April 6th, we completed our vision board and started praying for her exactly nine months to the day from her birthday! And then I remembered how she "caused" her birth to happen on that day, remembered that her heartrate was very low but she was in no danger. What we believe is that she caused the pain that sent her birth mother to the clinic for them to find the low heartrate so that she would be delivered on that day, giving us our sign that she had chosen us to be her parents!

Our takeaway from this was that vision boards not only work, but they work in perfect divine order just as God works in our own lives. We set the intention, used constant affirmative prayer, and remained open to however God wanted to grow our family. We couldn't be happier and are so grateful for our "spiritual pregnancy" and for the daughter we have now but also amazed that she is completely healthy despite her very challenging start. God is good all the time!

Secret Poem

Joe Green

Let's get extremely close.

Let's not be afraid of the closeness.

Let's pray together…

just once, informally.

And let's say I love you out loud

for the first time ever.

Let's not be afraid of the results.

Let's take a chance and do it.

Let's thank God for our health.

Let's respect our differences

And capitalize on our similarities.

It's been too long now.

And one of us may be gone tomorrow.

We have the power to end misconception.

I know we are grown now,

and shy....

But I do love you.

A Greater Love

Reverend Richard Burdick

An old Spanish proverb says, *"Where there is love, there is pain."* Whether that is true or not, I'm not sure, but I do know that "Where there is pain, there is always the opportunity to discover a greater love." I was called at one point in my life to demonstrate that greater love. A love I did not know existed within me.

I have no biological children, choosing instead to support, love, and nurture foster children. Suzie and I ran a group home where we raised kids who had been severely abused, "emotionally disturbed" and labeled by society as "broken". It was a rewarding job but one that at times was emotionally, financially and spiritually draining. In many instances, it would have been easier to walk away, but our sacred vow to love these kids always prevailed. True to our promise, we forced ourselves to find a deeper love that transcended any drain. I thank each of those young souls for the countless ways they blessed and challenged me and for a wife who walked the journey with me.

Each time we felt backed into the proverbial "corner" we dug deep into untapped reservoirs of love that transcended the difficulty and pain, both ours and the kids'. Sometimes hitting bottom is what helps us realize that love is the only thing we need. As it turned out, these kids were not broken at all. I believe we were all brought together as family to be "broken open" to a deeper expression of the vast miracle of love. Love opens us up when we are least expecting it.

Suzie and I ended up adopting three of these children. One of these kids was named Adam. Adam came to us a very angry, rage-filled boy who had been severely neglected by alcoholic parents who had lost their rights. Adam had, to say the least, a lot of challenges. During his seven years with us, Adam grew to be emotionally and spiritually healthy. I was a proud papa full of joy and hope for my son. Suzie and I loved Adam with all our hearts and although he loved us in return, he had a longing in his heart for his biological father. Out of our deep love for him, we facilitated brief visitations with his dad. Unfortunately, there was a hole in his heart that could not be filled by short visits.

While Adam was getting healthy, by some miracle so was his dad. He had freed himself from the grasp of alcohol and pulled his life together. He attributed much of his healing to our willingness to allow him to have a relationship with Adam. Over time Adam's counselor recommended that we allow him extended time with his dad and maybe even an occasional overnight visit. As his adoptive father and the one who had invested so much into Adam's wellbeing, this was very difficult. It threatened my ego to the core. Out of a love that is more powerful than fear and ego, we came to an agreement that it would be good for Adam to have a better connection with his biological dad.

The visits went well. Unfortunately, the better the visits went, the more Adam acted out in anger at home. He didn't seem to have the ability to love us *and* feel loyal to his biological father. It became clear that something needed to shift. The counselor eventually suggested that Adam move home with Bob and recommended that we rescind our adoptive parental rights. Painful? Yes. I had never heard of reversing an adoption before and it cut me to the marrow of my bones. *"Where there is pain there is the opportunity to discover a greater love."* I had to dig deep to find it. My vow was to always provide the very best for this young man so out of love we packed up his bags, full of so many beautiful memories and drove him home.

This was one of the most difficult things I have ever had to do in my life. Adam was my son, but there was a greater love that filled the hole in his heart in a way that I could not. Sometimes love hurts. Sometimes love causes agonizing pain and sometimes that pain is exactly what is needed for a greater love to emerge. It did. Adam and his dad thrived. They grew to be a very happy and healthy family. Love healed Adam, love healed his dad and although it was a slow process, love eventually healed my loss and grief.

Each of us is going to have opportunities to move through personal discomfort, fear and difficulty to demonstrate a God as love that is truly at the heart of every true spiritual aspirant. No one said it would be easy, but it is worth the journey.

We lost touch with Adam for many years but always longed to reconnect. Unfortunately, all our efforts to track him down left us empty handed and with a hole in our hearts wondering if he was okay. We gave up our search many years ago.

This past Thanksgiving, I received a Facebook message from a balding, bespectacled 32-year-old man who wanted to express his love and gratitude for the two people who gave him the strength, love and care he needed to become the man he was today. Looking through eyes filled with tears, I knew instantly this was the son I longed to know again. He had lost his childlike glow and innocence but there was no mistaking that this was the boy we had tucked in every night with the Unity Prayer of Protection. This was the son I had coached in baseball, wrestled with, played with, cried with, laughed with, camped with and held as we walked through so many moments of difficulty and celebration. No matter how painful life might be, in the end, love will always prevail.

At Unity North, I am grateful to be part of a community that demonstrates this truth every moment. To be surrounded with people who are committed to seeing beyond the veil of human experience is among my greatest blessings. UNA is a collection of "angels with skin on" that reminds me that if I look deeply enough I will always find the face of God. It is a family that helps me remember that if I listen carefully enough, the still small voice of God is always there. God bless Unity North; it has a way of guiding us home to the truth: no matter the pain, there is always the possibility of a greater love.

Safe Landing
Dixie Smith

Although I moved to Jacksonville, Florida in 2013 and attend and work at the Unity Church for Creative Living here, Unity North Atlanta Church will always feel like home. I am so grateful for the years I spent there and am often aware of all the gifts I received at UNA!

I found UNA when my twins were nearing their teen years. Having older children, I knew how difficult it could be in the teens and wanted so much for Chris and Kristen to be exposed to spirituality. I was adamant that they not attend a church where they were told that a particular denomination had all the "right" answers and everyone else was wrong. And I knew that I didn't believe in the angry, vindictive God so many people still worship.

I attended a few churches, and had seen UNA on Sandy Plains Road when my good friend, Deb McGhie, suggested I give it a try. I went once without my kids or husband, and felt immediately at home. There was a sense of peace and acceptance that I hadn't found anywhere else. The next week, the kids and husband came, too, and we were hooked.

When I first began to attend church there, I chose not to join anything right away. I didn't know all about what Unity taught, and I just wanted to be fed and nurtured for a while. One of my first Sundays there, the minister said these words, "You may not agree with everything you hear, and that's okay, what we teach is different than what you may have heard before. I just encourage you to take the time to consider what you hear and embrace whatever part of it that feels right to you." That is exactly what I did and what a joy it was to be "given permission" to use my own brain, heart and intuition. It wasn't long before I was sold on the Unity Principles and ready to be involved.

In the course of my dozen years at UNA, I learned many things. The most important is that every idea is a Divine idea. If there's something you feel led to do, don't be afraid to do it. It may not turn out exactly as you expect, but something wonderful will come out of the effort you make. In the course of these years, as I developed the philosophy I wrote about in my first book, *Just Say "Yes!"*, I discovered that when I put forth the intention of serving Spirit, ideas and opportunities came. My idea was to recognize opportunities that came my way as being part of the Divine plan, and to say "Yes!" instead of the usual knee jerk reaction of, "No way, I couldn't possibly do that." My plan was to agree to do anything that wasn't illegal, immoral or against my personal code of ethics. I've found when I say "Yes!" to opportunities, I inevitably find that I have more ability than I imagined.

What a journey it's been! I was often nervous as I was asked to do things I wasn't sure I could do, but in every case just when I felt that the tasks I accepted were too big, I would get an email or an offhand comment from someone that would keep me going. "Dixie, I really enjoyed your article; I needed to hear that!" "Your singing touched me today." "I remember what you said two years ago about just saying 'Yes!' and it has changed my life." I never thought I could be an inspiration to anyone. What I have learned, though, is that we ALL can be.

So many opportunities I've had have been because of my connection to Unity North. I started to sing in the Choir and Don Discenza suggested some of us put together small groups to sing backup. That's where the trio, Full Circle, came from. I joined a small group and after attending for a year or so, was asked to lead the group. I didn't think I could do it. My friend who had been the leader, Marie Reynolds, was so graceful at dealing with people and an amazing meditator and leader. I checked my criteria, and it wasn't illegal, immoral or against my personal code of ethics, so I sighed, but I said "Yes." I learned so much from stepping into those shoes that I never knew I needed to know.

A couple of years later, I accepted the challenge to become a Prayer Chaplain, and learned that I could pray out loud. And I grew in my understanding of integrity, non-judgment and holding space for the highest and best outcome for all. In my first year, I was asked to take the Prayer Chaplain Trainer training and became the leader of the Prayer Chaplains. I was honored to be asked, and learned so much as a result of accepting this challenge.

A mother of five, I NEVER thought I'd work with teens but when that opportunity came, I said "Yes!" and I am now the Southeast Unity Ministries Y.O.U. Consultant, helping to plan rallies for 14 to 18 year olds as well as trainings and retreats for adults.

I said "Yes!" to moving to Jacksonville, and now I find that my life is rich and full; I'm in a position here as YFM Director to use so much of what I learned in my years at UNA. I learned from every minister and congregant I experienced there. I learned to love myself and that forgiving myself allows me to forgive others. I learned that things happen FOR me and not TO me. And so much more. I am not sure what the next few years will bring, but I'm thankful every day that I landed at UNA. And I never discount the possibility that one day I may be back! I love the congregation of Unity North!

Journey of Gratitude
Tom Ballinger

My first exposure to UNA was the Wednesday night of holy week in 2000. Doreen Virtue was there and was amazing. Carole's presence as host was positive and promised spiritual growth. We attended Sunday services the following Sunday and Don's jazz closed the deal. We had looked for a spiritual community for a while and found UNA resonated deeply with us. We were home.

We became members in the fall of 2000 when my daughter started attending the Uniteens. Since becoming members I have been active in the choir, sound team, chaplains, Conscious Living Circles (CLCs), men's group, and chaperoned several Youth of Unity (Y.O.U) rallies.

Early on, Carole relayed the metaphysical interpretation of the Bible's phrase "...judge not and be not judged" which is all judgment is self- judgment. This interpretation has caused years of growth: insights to myself and others which helped me understand and via that understanding, find compassion.

Realizing whenever I felt fear, or a manifestation of fear, was an opportunity to grow and was a huge breakthrough for me. The emotion was the vehicle I have used to gain insight into myself and start unravelling my subconscious programing. The first few years of my internal journey contained a number of tough lessons reminding me of the phrase: sometime it takes a 2X4.

As I have grown I have been able to apply what I learned about myself to others. Learning to quickly realize when someone is reacting through fear and through that understanding, feel compassion. Everything you say, think, feel, or do has nothing to do with anyone or anything but you.

Attending, hosting and facilitating CLCs for about 15 years has taught me how to listen to others, hearing heart and body, not just their words. Being present for someone is a sign of respect. And being listened to by others who are present, when expressing your thoughts and ideas on various questions, grows a feeling of worthiness and trust.

UNA has offered me the tools to start the process of awakening. Once this process has started, it cannot be stopped. I thank UNA and everyone I have met at UNA for helping me to learn who I am.

The Long Way Home
Nita Roberts

As soon as I tell people that from birth to marriage, I attended a small church deep in Georgia's piney-woods and that my ancestors had been attending that same church since 1884, I watch their eyes and wait for the questions to begin. "Speaking in tongues? Fire and brimstone?? SNAKE HANDLERS?" I smile coyly and trot out a story about church-going southern style. I make brimstones grow into white hot boulders while serpents writhe in the pulpit guided by a faux Burt Lancaster/Elmer Gantry. After I've had my fun, I finally say that in truth, there were no snakes to handle at Palmetto Methodist Church (at least not during the 50s and 60s), no hell fires, and the only language spoken was Southern. My listener's attention falters. The tale deflates, and I have to admit that for a storyteller's purpose, my church experiences were tame fodder, darn it!

Church services were held twice a week. Vacation Bible School was every June, and smack in the dead heat of the Georgia summer, there was "Revival" time. Revival meant sitting outside on folding chairs or quilts, dinner on long tables under a shed cover, guitar and fiddle music, and preaching from a visiting minister. We all knew his aim was to get us to reconnect ourselves more firmly with God. And we'd try to hold out to the bitter end, maybe because it was so hot and we were feeling churlish. But by the fourth singing of "Just As I Am" the Holy Spirit would get under our feet, fly us up into the warmth and light around that visiting preacher and we'd vow to be better neighbors, better Christians.

The messages from my church were simple: believe in God, be a good neighbor, share what you have, don't be a Willful Wanter but rather a Grateful Receiver, pray, and when you make a mistake, fix it as best you can and then go on, wiser.

I went away to college, married, and moved to Roswell where my new in-laws were founding members of the Episcopal Church. I really wanted everything to fit for me there, family tradition and all that. But there was so much standing up, sitting down, crouching on the seat edge, Prayer Books and Call and Response, I became dizzy. I imagined wearing a too tight spiritual girdle. After a year or two, I knew that being a good Episcopalian was not going to work for me.

My then husband and I bought a boat and a lake house. He and I reasoned that we were communing with God-created nature and that would be enough, but it was not enough, not for me. There was a hole in my heart that I could usually dance around but on occasion, would fall into. It was a dark and lonely place. I knew I needed a church home again with messages that rang true.

I began talking to people about their churches. The Morman church sounded interesting. But all that stockpiling of wives and food seemed a bit excessive. Baptist? Being "saved" was a lot more than just letting the Holy Spirit lead one to a place of warmth and light and there was trickiness involved in their "Being Saved" plan. I wasn't so sure about that whole Hell thing. Fine for them but I needed to move on.

I hoped the local Methodist Church might get me back to my roots. Unfortunately, my visit coincided with that of the Gideon Society's representative. Perhaps I'd read one too many Friedan or Steinem books but really, what self-respecting woman could sit still to hear "our women serve on their knees so their men can walk"? Now tell me, is that the way one neighbor treats another? No one else seemed to mind. Moving on again.

I seemed to fit no place and no place fit me. Where were the simple, true messages I remembered from my childhood?

My friend, Forrest, was on her own quest for a church home. She called saying there was a woman, a minister who talked about attracting energy. We laughed. Were kites, strings, keys and dangerous thunderstorms involved? We decided to go listen, once. Couldn't hurt, probably. And we did. And then we went again. And again. Forrest and I listened carefully. We took notes, we went to classes, and we read the books Reverend Carole mentioned in her talks all the while staring at her from the front row with our big eyes. Forrest and I began noticing how things Reverend Carole suggested we try, began working in our lives. There was something old and familiar woven into those new words. I began feeling that I was finding my home again.

Reverend Carole retired. Occasionally, Reverend Richard, our Youth Director, would step in and deliver the Sunday message as new ministers vying for Reverend Carole's position flowed into and then out of our church. There were financial issues, dissention. I felt Unity North gently but noticeably swaying. I was afraid and forgot to trust that we were in our perfect space. I left and gave my heart to a new start-up church. *Traitor!* I worked hard there and tried to follow what I thought was a new path being revealed. Eventually, I realized that for me, this path was off my course. I felt nudges that became harder and harder to ignore. I wanted to return to Unity but I had disappointed my Unity neighbors by leaving. I was ashamed.

Reverend Richard became the full-time minister. I remembered hearing the same truth in his words as I had from Reverend Carole. But, could I go back?

It was hard going through Unity's double doors. I tried to slip in unnoticed but familiar faces saw me, responded in surprise ... but with warmth. So far, so good. Reverend Richard was walking the aisles greeting people before the service. I kept my head down and pretended to read the bulletin, word by word. I saw his shoes stop in front of my chair. Why did I sit at the end of the row? He was waiting. It was very hard to look up, afraid of what I'd see. *Traitor!* But I did not see "Traitor" in his eyes; he was smiling. I remember standing up as best I could and softly saying I'd made a mistake in leaving. He said, quite simply, "Well then, welcome back home!"

Sunday Morning

Suzie Burdick

This was a blue sky, sunny morning, sparkling and clean...

A dancing leaf, shouting hallelujah kind of morning...

A wind ruffled, shadow tossing, orange juice and toast morning

Calling me to hurry with my work kind of morning or you'll be

late morning!

A yellow leafed, fly buzzing, lazy quiet road morning when it

seemed no one else was headed anywhere.

A thought stirring, soul reflecting, love sharing, friend caring

kind of morning and my thoughts turn to you morning.

For it was Sundays that our friendship met and grew.

"Blessed be the ties that bind our hearts..."

I Follow my Vision, I Follow it Through

Sara Crawford

*"If one advances confidently in the direction
of his dreams, and endeavors to live the life
which he has imagined, he will meet with a
success unexpected in common hours..."*

- *Henry David Thoreau*

New Year's Eve 2012: I was supposed to be in New Orleans, but (let's just say) *life happened,* and my trip got cut short. I decided I might as well go to the Burning Bowl ceremony since I was in town. I had been attending Unity North Atlanta Church off and on since 2007, but I hadn't attended in almost a year. The Burning Bowl was always my favorite service at Unity, and I figured I had a lot of *releasing* to do so I got in my car and drove down to the church.

As soon as I walked in, I heard Reverend Richard Burdick playing a soulful rendition of "Somewhere Over the Rainbow." I was immediately filled with a familiar comfort. In that moment, this place was my true sanctuary. *I was home.*

91

I had just completed my Master's degree in Creative Writing. I was 27 years old, completely broke, and living with my parents after I ran out of financial aid and had to give up my one-bedroom apartment. I had been in school in one form or another ever since I could remember, and I was no longer a student. It was time to actually *do something* with my life.

When I had attended Unity in the past, I sat in the sanctuary and enjoyed the talks. I felt inspired by the music. I even participated in a Conscious Living Circle group and briefly sang in the choir, but I had never *really* gotten involved. Being the awkward introvert that I am, I had never opened up to anyone there.

I noticed on the bulletin that they were having auditions for the musical, *Godspell*. Having been in a production 10 years earlier in a community theatre group, I was familiar with the show. But I had spent the last five or six years studying playwriting, and I hadn't actually performed in quite some time. (Unless you count the smoky dive bars I sang in with my band.)

I wrote down what I wanted to release from 2012, and I held it out to the fire, watching the flames consume my paper. I smiled and walked out of the church, ready to begin a new year, ready to figure out what the next chapter of my life would look like.

I auditioned for *Godspell* with a cover of "Dancing with Myself" by Billy Idol on my acoustic guitar. It was unconventional, but it earned me a spot in the cast. No matter how much of a shy, quiet person I was, I found it impossible to be in a production of *Godspell*—jumping and dancing around like clowns on acid as Jesus taught us about love, kindness, and peace in song—and not become a part of the community.

Things were starting to look up. I got an internet marketing job, I moved into a little bohemian apartment in the Marietta Square, and I completed my first young adult novel. *Godspell* was helping me to finally get involved with Unity, and I became a member of the church in February 2013.

Over the years, my experiences at Unity North have taught me invaluable lessons. I have learned about the importance of forgiveness and gratitude. I have learned about prayer and meditation, how to accept myself for who I am, and that God can be found *everywhere*: in the cracks in the sidewalk, in the crunching leaves on the ground in autumn, even in the eyes of those who have hurt me. I learned that I could change my thoughts and my life would change. And now I was learning how to let other people in Unity see me, too. But the most important thing that Unity North has taught me is how to stand in my own truth.

Fast forward to February 2014: I was almost 29. My young adult novel landed me a New York literary agent, and I started to put my degrees to good use—freelance editing and freelance writing on the side. And yet, I wasn't happy. I spent every weekday in a cold office, marketing other people's businesses, working to make other people's dreams come true.

When my boss left the company, I was offered a promotion. I would be the new marketing manager. I enjoyed the stability that my job provided, and yet, I knew in my heart that I wasn't standing in my own truth. I knew that my job no longer served me.

I prayed about it and meditated on it. I listened to Reverend Richard Burdick and Reverend Carole O'Connell as they encouraged the congregation to do what we were called to do, to face our fears and trust that God/the Universe would take care of the details. I led the congregation as a member of the worship team, singing, "*I follow my vision, I follow it through.*"

I decided to close my eyes and take a leap.

I quit my day job and started freelance writing, editing, and marketing full-time. It was risky. It was scary. I didn't know how everything was going to work out, but I trusted that it would. I was following the advice I had been singing to the congregation; I was following my vision.

Now, I work full-time from my home office, freelance editing manuscripts for other authors, writing blog posts and web content for various clients, and helping independent authors and educational organizations with marketing. It's been over a year since I "quit my day job" and I am thriving.

On a recent trip to New York, I was walking down Broadway looking at the flashing lights, on the way to meet my literary agent for the first time, and I couldn't help but pause for a moment and think about how truly blessed I am.

Unity North Atlanta has changed my life. I have been inspired and uplifted. I have learned how to appreciate obstacles and challenges for the lessons they teach. Some of the most significant relationships in my life are now with people I met at Unity. But most importantly, Unity North has given me the strength and faith to walk confidently in the direction of my dreams.

Unconditional Love
RoseMarie Pacella

As I was meditating, my journey started to unfold
One I never expected one that made me feel whole.

For my inner child appeared and shined so pure and bright
And in her eyes, I saw that everything was right.

She said, I have a secret and smiled; you are perfect, you see,
You were never broken, but were always complete.

Unconditional love did she impart to me, so real and alive
And then I heard her whispering, you are so special
For I've missed you, I've missed you,
You're the reflection of me.

Getting to the Good Part of Wonderful
Dr. Eugie Tindal-Kirkpatrick

"Not all who wander are lost."
- *J.R.R. Tolkien*

As I move between biology and cosmology, life provides a wonderful journey of winding paths, roads, hills, valleys and tunnels that present exciting escapes and experiences into a wonder of gigantic proportions. It's all wonderful!

Most of us, even with the best laid plans, find ourselves in wonder as we sometimes wander into new and unchartered places on our journey. Serendipitous surprises sometime show up in the places least expected as we do our best to navigate our lives.

My intention is to see and live a life of wonder, to create my own path into fulfilling, adventurous and new experiences. My journey is constantly unfolding from within me as I "join the journey within" at Unity North Atlanta Church.

During this season of my life, I am enjoying what I refer to as "the good part of wonderful". The appreciation of good increases and multiplies the good available to all. In my honest opinion, knowing and growing in the goodness of life as intended by our Creator is organic for all of humankind.

For me, Unity North Atlanta led to a paradise of the soul. I awoke to an atmosphere where love was everywhere, where people were infused with an insatiable appetite for authentic living and activities that enlightened the spirit, soul and body. The oneness of all creation is evident and accepted with grace. I know that I have discovered "the good part of wonderful" right here and right now.

Unity North Atlanta is a beautiful microcosm of the panoramic garden of God where life thrives and the energy of ecstatic existence is pervasive. As I live my own "a la carte" life and choose from a vast menu of good that I desire and experience, Unity North provides for me a reflection of my internal self: the good and the holy, the fun and the fantastic, the joyful and adventurous. Unity North allows me to vicariously experience worlds of divergent religious rituals and spiritual paths, philosophies, and colorful expressions of foreign places which I have read and taught about. Through Unity North, I have traveled fantastically into the vast worlds of my own vivid imagination!

The countless ministries, events, classes, and activities orchestrated and conducted by the phenomenal, anointed, and talented leadership of the church are like the harmonious sounds of a musical composition that invites all to join in the wonderful and exciting dance.

Unity North Atlanta for me is one of the best parts of my wonderful wandering in this amazing season of my life as I continue my journey of enlightenment, friendship, expansion, and joyful exploration! For this, and in all of this, I give sincere thanks to God and to my Unity North family and community. I know that the goodness unearthed within me is excavated from within the deep realms of my soul and my being now and will be so throughout all eternity.

I truly am wandering, but I am not lost. I have found exactly what I have been looking for in the journey within, which is also the journey within Unity North Atlanta!

Thank you, Unity North Atlanta!

The Third Way

Rose Anita Renner

We see a fork in the road,
    any pathway choice in life.
A choice must always be made.
    Should we go left or go right?

But stop let us look again.
    In the shadow of the light,
in the middle between them,
    a narrow way lies in sight.

Now when given two choices,
    slow down, light of truth do sense.
the narrow path is hidden.
    For those who can see look hence.

The third way will prove utmost,
    the pathway of the seeker.
Journey safely round the curves.
    Your life is yours, consider.

Sometimes I Wonder
Joe Green

Do you ever wonder? Do you ever think about why everything you think about becomes your life? Be careful what you think about. You get to choose. Anything you think about comes back to you.

I don't know the exact moment when it happened, but about 20 years ago I was led to a local church that was similar yet very different from my Methodist upbringing. My first visit was with a small gathering of people calling themselves Unity. They were meeting temporarily at the historic Naylor House in Roswell, Georgia, and they were looking for a church home. Little did I know I would soon become a grateful part of that new church home.

There was no specific profound event that lured me to Unity, nor was there one magical epiphany that kept me coming. It just felt right from the start with the simple message of oneness, love, non-judgment, the power of thought, and the realization that I was a personal expression of Christ through all my thoughts and actions. I wanted to grow further and I soon knew I had found my new spiritual home…and here I am 20 years later.

The power of thought has always guided my life long before I heard the Unity principles. I'm a dreamer and have always lived knowing the one omnipotent thought is Love: seek it, embrace it, live it, share it. I suppose that is why Unity fits me so well. This simple mantra of "Dream it, Plan it, Do it" has blessed me beyond words. The basic straightforward message to love God, honor all, judge not, and pray endlessly has given me a wonderful peace and confidence to live by.

Through Unity, I believe in the message of Jesus, and I believe that God is within me, not outside of me. I believe there is only one God, and this God presence opens all doors if I am willing to enter them. There's much I don't know or understand but I remain at peace knowing my church community is there for me, a loving place where I can both serve and receive.

I don't know why my life has been so blessed
　　　　but I SING about everything
I don't know who made God,
　　　　but I SMILE a very long while.
I don't know what tomorrow will bring,
　　　　but I DANCE and take another chance.
I don't know if I'll live another day,
　　　　but I LAUGH for my own behalf.

I DO know prayer is power and so I BREATHE energy.

I DO know thoughts precede action so I CREATE my masterpiece.

I DO know nature is God's paintbrush,

   so I EXPLORE far beyond my back door.

I DO know love is the key, and so I LOVE endlessly.

And if this all just seems
too simple to believe.
It's inside you and me
and it's beyond your wildest dreams.

Thank you Unity North Atlanta for teaching me, nurturing me, guiding me, and accepting me as I am. I pray I can continue to give back just as I have received here.

I am an Unstoppable Force
Sylvia Hopper

I found Unity the way many people do, in times of great need. I married husband number one while a freshman at Memphis State having dated him for three years in high school. I am and have always been a female Don Quixote, tilting at windmills all over, but never with such life changing consequences as this time.

I grew up as an involved member of the local Methodist church in a town where anyone not a member of the Church of Christ was bound for real estate called "Hell." They had a ministerial school in my hometown and attempts at saving my mortal soul were a regular occurrence in my life. At that time in my soul's evolution, my understanding of God was like many others' today, except that perhaps my personal relationship was one of a pact made with that all knowing entity in which I did as I thought "he" wanted me to do and in return my life was supposed to go as I had envisioned. You can only imagine my shock when things did not go according to plan.

In my new home, with my new husband, Joe, there lived a father-in-law who was a very prejudiced and mean-spirited individual. On the day in question, he told the maid, Lular, a tiny, sweet, African American lady not to touch his hat. At the time, she was already holding his hat while dusting under it, and she dropped it as quickly as she had picked it up. He slapped her, knocking her thin body to the floor. Before I had time to think, my hand, which appeared to have a mind of its own, came around and slapped the old man to the floor. I was both shocked and speechless and just stared at my hand. Of course, my days were numbered in that marriage.

I had mono and spent a few weeks in bed. My father-in-law cursed me daily, calling me every name he could. Finally, the doctor told my husband that I could not survive much less get well in that house. My husband took me to my mother. Can you imagine?

After six weeks of being bedridden, I crawled to the phone and called him. He said simply, "I want a divorce." I drove to the house in my shortie pajamas with a raincoat as a cover-up and confronted him.

He said, "Daddy says it's me or you. Looks like it's going to be you!"

I calmly walked into the bedroom and took the gun from the bed, placed it to my temple and pulled the trigger. The safety was on, and when it clicked, both Joe and Lular ran into the room as I was attempting to turn off the safety. Joe knocked the gun from my hand and it flew across the room. Both went down on their knees and I remember telling them to get up.

Now comes the pact with God. How dare he leave me and break our "contract!" I drove to the Methodist Church, marched into the minister's office in my lovely outfit with the coat hanging open and said, "You and the Methodist Church can go straight to Hell!"

I then took my whole $40 and the few clothes I had in an old suitcase and caught a bus to Memphis to a father I did not know. Now here is where God really stepped up and I found myself on a road as a student of the truth. My father was married to a Unity Student who changed my life forever. She became the mother that was given to me to make up for all of the terrible things that have ever occurred in my life before or since. She taught me that if I don't like what is happening to me, that all I have to do is change me and my thinking, the rest takes care of itself. It's a job for God, that power in the universe that is in all and through all and in which we all move and have our being.

I joined Unity at the ripe old age of 21 in Memphis. I have learned that life is forever unfolding as it should, not always as we expect it or want it to be. I am now 74 with 53 years in the movement, and I can honestly say it saved my life. When I removed husband number two, Bill, from the house, I called Jay Dishman, my then minister of 20 years.

"Jay, I am afraid for Bill," I said. "I just kicked him out and I fear for his life."

"Sylvia, have you ever been able to fall beneath the love of your God?" he asked.

"Of course not!"

"I am confused, do you and Bill have different Gods?" he said. "I rest my case."

I can relate hundreds of stories along the way, but the threads that are constant are my unwavering trust in my God, my faith in things unseen and my joy in living. Husband number two was an alcoholic and a manic-depressive, and 14 years with him gave me many opportunities for growth. It was a karmic relationship where I got to make up for the way I treated him last time and truly understand forgiveness from all angles, to turn the other cheek. "Judge not lest you be judged" takes on a whole new meaning when you spend three months of each year visiting your husband in a mental ward. He was a tortured soul and did the best he could.

My father left when I was very young, and he too was an alcoholic. He burned himself in an accident, and I went to see him on Christmas Day. He told me he loved me as much as he could on his deathbed, and I realized this was the first time he told me he loved me.

Doesn't sound like much of a life to be joyful over, does it? But let me tell you, I have touched so many lives with my boundless love. I am a wife, mother, and grandmother. I have loved and been loved by so many souls. It doesn't get much better than this!

My grandmother, Mammy, played a vital role in my life. Mammy didn't attend a church. I remember coming come from school one day in tears and telling her that no one would ever know I had been here.

Mammy said, "What are you talking about girl? You can have anything in the world you want. Just know there is a price for everything. Negotiate the price up front, be willing to pay it, and go for it with all the gusto in your body and nothing on earth can stop you. You my darling are an unstoppable force!"

Do you think Mammy might just have been a closet Truth Student? I bought it, my Mammy's belief, and I have had an amazing life as the unstoppable force I became at my Mammy's feet.

It doesn't matter how you get on a path or what that path looks like, as long as you are on one. We are never "there." We just keep on keeping on. I have had so many wonderful experiences that I could have seen as bad, and I am so blessed and thankful for this wonderful journey called Unity!

Finding Unity North Atlanta, Restoring Myself
Maryann Hopper

Back in the 1990s when I worked with my friend, Donna, she often told me how inspired she was by attending Unity North Atlanta Church, but I kept putting off her invitations to "meet the people." I hadn't attended church since the 1960s.

When I was a teenager, my Methodist minister was driven from our small town church by the church board when he welcomed the poor into our sanctuary. That was my first recognition that some live by their spiritual convictions when confronted with a challenge to the status quo, and others take refuge in priorities they deem for the "good" of the church. After that experience, I went to the library in search of spiritual knowledge. I chose the study of philosophy and religion as an intellectual exercise. I moved in and out of many organized religious circles, always warily looking for the truth, yet taking care to protect my spiritual feelings and my newly emerging lesbian identity.

I found that churches had nothing to offer me except "love the sinner, hate the sin," so I didn't consider returning.

My spiritual life was confined to reading feminist theologians who were attempting to make changes for women from within the church, yet exclusionary doctrine is slow to change. To find support and solace, I found the lesbian underground full of social, political, and spiritual activities held in our own "safe" places. My life was a search for worthiness, acceptance, and equality.

In the late 1990s, Donna moved away, limiting our time of spirited discussions to phone chats, and in 2003, I retired. I began to think about the changes retirement would bring, that I would need to create a new kind of life for my senior years. Also I wanted to expand my friendships beyond co-workers and political activists.

Since my partner, Drea, was bitter about her past encounters with religion, I decided to slip into church one Sunday in early 2004 by myself to hear what Unity North was about. The bright sun illuminated the sanctuary. The natural world was still visible. I felt lighter already. I looked around and didn't know a soul, but people were friendly and dressed in whatever seemed comfortable to them. The musicians were engaging, their music modern, lively, and the words were new to me, but I could relate to their messages. Reverend Carole O'Connell was REAL, her authenticity amazing, and her message heartfelt. During "sharing and caring" congregants

opened up about their joys and their needs. People listened.
The environment felt amazingly welcoming.

When I returned, sometimes there were guest speakers
and different singers that stretched my expectations. I loved
uncovering the story of Myrtle and Charles Fillmore, the Unity
founders, who lived their beliefs. I wanted to trust again that
the spiritual message that I heard on Sundays was really being
embraced by the congregants. As time passed, I did find the
friends that I was seeking at Unity North, and I wanted to be a
part of this movement.

Today our spiritual leader, Reverend Richard Burdick,
continues to keep our spiritual energy high by sharing his
honest and earnest messages. And our environment is a caring
one that I have settled into.

When I leave Unity North, I never feel that I'm a sinner
who has to make amends or someone defective because I am a
lesbian. Instead I am assured that I am a spiritual being that
constantly is given a new lease on life, a new path to try. All
paths lead to God reverberates in my mind. I enjoy returning to
activities during the week as well as on Sunday to learn many
ways to step into a positive outlook and to be reminded that
life is good. Now I extend this enlightenment into my daily life
and in my conversations with others. At Unity North, I often
hear of stimulating new thought books and seek them out in

our bookstore. I am constantly challenged to expand my consciousness.

This phase of my life is filled with joy and creativity, words I rarely heard during my many years within corporate workplaces or outside them as well. My life continues to unfold with opportunities for spiritual growth in every part of my existence. It's hard to remember that my vocabulary used to be filled with defensive words and a focus only on battling oppression that came with my lesbian lifestyle. I am happy to be accepted for who I really am, a spiritual being.

I listen with my heart to the messages of oneness with all beings. This is an internal growth, a silent acknowledgement that my Spirit swims inside the same ether as all other beings. Unity has helped me integrate my life into a spiritual whole. I grow less wary of discovering a caveat condemning lesbians in Unity's church doctrine or in Unity's special classes. I know you have to open yourself to be a part of an accepting community, and I am willing.

Initially, I hoped that whatever contributions I could make would be welcomed. And they were. I met accepting people when I helped with Kidsmas, with summer kids' camp, with the soldier boxes, the coat drives, the Rainbow garden, and countless fundraisers including the *Red Tent* Movie that my partner, Drea, and our Crones Council organized at Unity. I've joined prayer groups, enjoyed women's retreats, musical performances, inspiring guest speakers, holiday gatherings surrounded by people that I mostly feel comfortable being with, counting on that we are all "on the spiritual path" and most of the time, we are on it together.

The Intrepid Leaf

Sharon Allen-Peterson

One day as I began my daily walk, I saw the most interesting thing. It was a leaf that looked like an undercover operative, all covered in leafy vestments, inching its way along a bustling avenue.

The leaf was covered beneath another leaf. It looked like it was trying to cross a big road as it continued on its most secret mission. The funny thing was that the leaf appeared to be scuttling along—almost as if it was being followed, as it stuck out of its leafy cover-up every few steps. And, no, it was not just the way it moved that made it stand out, but also how it wove in and out of the street traffic avoiding all potential pedestrians.

There were fishermen preparing their boats to catch seafood to sell when they come in from the day's work, and fruit and vegetable stands where people could buy oranges and mangos and strawberries or other fruits and vegetables for sale. It was a beautiful day and everyone seemed to be enjoying a minute or two to talk to the others they met along the way...*except* the leaf. Whatever his mission, he took it very seriously and worked at a rather fast pace to accomplish his tasks.

Perhaps the leaf was on its way to a rendezvous at the local theatre or was trying to avoid notice by the undercover police marshals that patrolled the waterfront that led to the big ocean? Whatever his mission he seemed persistent, and I say this because, this small, fragile piece of nature had a definite purpose for his stealthy agenda.

Just as I noticed out of the corner of my vision some movement near the leaf, I saw a little piece of the leaf's outer covering slip, and I got a view of what was underneath the shell of the covering and it looked like a…wait a minute, I'm not sure but I think, oh, could it be? I got closer to the leaf and saw a chrysalis emerging from its cocoon. I was speechless as this beautiful butterfly gracefully tested her wings and erupted with new life in all its wonder, soon soaring as if this is what she had been waiting for, and indeed it was!

I'm not sure how the leaf knew what was happening, but that is the mystery and belief that we humans may never know. As the new butterfly flew by, the leaf skittered closer to the butterfly, as if to say, good luck! The butterfly revved up her wings and wrote with cloud dust: Thanks for protecting me while I was growing. I will never forget your kindness.

Love Day

Rainy Suggs

Over the last four years at Unity North, I have had so many valuable lessons and experiences that have been life changing, but there is one experience that stands out in my mind more than the rest.

It was Valentine's Day 2013. I woke up that morning feeling a little down, as I am sure many single Americans do on this beloved couples holiday. I got up, got dressed, and headed into work. I remember listening to the radio with all of the ads for jewelry shops, flowers, and candy as they announced promotions of events for couples to attend, and I couldn't help but feel very alone. Then it hit me; I remembered there was a Valentine's Day dance at Unity North. I knew I didn't have anyone to go with as a date, but I knew they needed volunteers. I figured this year instead of focusing on not yet having that special someone in my life, I would focus on giving other people love. I wasn't going to let not having a date stop me from spending time with my church family that I love so dearly. So, I called the church immediately and asked if I could help in any way. Of course they said they would love to have me work the door and greet people as they entered the dance. My mood instantly began to shift.

I got to work and walked into my office and found a Valentine's gift from my co-worker. All week we had decided to celebrate #LoveWeek which was created by MindValley for employees to show love and appreciation to each other the week of Valentine's Day. When I saw my gift, another shift began to occur for me: I realized that I wasn't alone, I had great co-workers who loved and appreciated me. I had a church full of people who loved and appreciated me and who I loved and appreciated. The feeling of loneliness began to fade. I remembered that at Unity we believe God is love. Then one of my co-workers walked by and said, "Happy Love Day", and that was when the magic happened for me.

I replied "Happy Love Day," and I instantly felt a total shift in my body. I felt lighter, I was smiling from ear to ear, and I felt full of love. By changing one little word the greeting took on a whole new feeling and meaning for me. I had to try this again, so I got up and went to each of my co-workers office's and instead of the usual "Happy Valentine's Day" I greeted them with "Happy Love Day" and each and every time, each person was a little caught off guard, but lit up with a smile and replied "Happy Love Day!" I could see the energy shift in each person. Then it hit me. If I could change my day by just changing one word, I could possibly do that for each and every person that walked through the doors of our church that night.

I got back to my office and went on with my day. When five o'clock came I raced out the door. I couldn't wait to get to Unity and share my new revelation with everyone I greeted at the door.

When I arrived at church, one of my best friends was there to volunteer as well. He too was having some of the same feelings I had been having earlier in the day. I shared with him my revelation and that I wanted to greet everyone at the door with "Happy Love Day" instead of "Happy Valentine's Day." People began arriving and when we began saying "Happy Love Day," something magical happened! Each person would stop, pause, then smile and say "Happy Love Day" back! I watched each person's entire body, mind and spirit shift. It made me shift. I saw people light up. By changing one word, we changed their whole night, and for some their outlook on the holiday. Valentine's Day was no longer about expectations or gifts. It was just about love. Unity North taught me that our thoughts, words, and actions create our lives. I also learned that love is truly the most powerful force we have.

In the end, I realized just how truly powerful our words can be. I finally understood. All it takes is one word and our lives can be changed forever. For better or worse. The true gift is that we are always at choice with not only our words but also everything in our lives. Thanks to Unity North, I now choose "Love."

The Promise (Ode to Your Life)
Michael March

The promise of tomorrow is alive with us today,
Our yesterdays should be cherished, but only the present
should hold sway.
Carpe diem, a translation from the Latin beseeches us to seize
the day.

Why wait to see what the future brings; what might be in store.
It is up to each one of us to love, to cherish and adore.
No rudderless ship lost and floundering at sea, or lack of
rowers to guide it to shore.

United we stand, eyes focused and minds extremely clear,
The belief we share protects us and teaches us to have no fear.

No pledges broken or un-kept promises to be made.
With the Lord as our inspiration, our faith will never fade.

So thank you for your guidance and outpouring of your love.
Heaven is within us all, not just waiting for the select, so very
high above.

Share the promise of friendship, kindness and understanding
with all you meet,
And thank the spirit that fills us for his unconditional love,
because life is so sweet.

Coming Home to Unity
Lynn Phillips

My grandmother was my primary source of spiritual
inspiration when I was growing up. While my parents were
quite conventional, my grandmother was a mystic, whose
apartment was filled with literature as wide ranging as Science
of Mind and Vedanta, to books by various swamis, yogis, and
even Mary Baker Eddy. When I was a small child, she taught
me "There is one power and presence in the universe – and
that is God. There is no place God is not, and God is Love."
She also taught me a prayer that she said was the most
important prayer I would ever pray, and we said it together
every day. That prayer is the one we know as the prayer of
protection. "The Light of God surrounds us; the Love of God
enfolds us; the Power of God protects us; the Presence of God
watches over us. Wherever we are, God is." She didn't talk
about the Unity Church, and I didn't know it existed.

I visited many churches and temples and read
extensively about various religions as an adult, but none quite
fit my deeply-held beliefs about the nature of reality (our
Oneness, our essential unity, the profound sense that God is
the field in which we live and move and exist, and God is in us)
and none of the conventional churches taught about Jesus as an

121

example of any of this. I didn't want to worship him but rather to live the life that he said we should live. I visited monasteries and even mystical groups meeting in homes, but none really resonated with me. I resigned myself to meditation and affirmational prayer at home to strengthen my spiritual path, rather than attending a group of any sort.

Fast forward to 1991, long after my grandmother passed over. I was driving down Johnson Ferry Road in Marietta, GA one day in October, and I saw a sign outside a shopping center for a store front church. It said "Homecoming this Sunday," and I felt compelled to attend that homecoming. There was nothing special about the sign – no neon or special message, yet it spoke to something deep within me. Yes, it was Unity North Atlanta. We sang the Prayer of Protection, and when I heard the words aloud that I had only spoken in my mind since my grandmother passed, the joy I felt was indescribable. The philosophy and message matched my belief system. We even meditated together for a few minutes! It was indeed a homecoming: coming home to Unity.

Playing Attention
Jay Scholfield

Signs are everywhere. They come in all shapes, sizes and wave lengths. It's up to us, the "messagee" to "play attention" … as my dear ol' Dad used to say! My journey into greater consciousness began some 10 years ago. I was driving down Sandy Plains Road in a funky state of mind during a turbulent time in my life, and I saw up ahead, of course, on the "right" side of the road, a sign that read "Unity North Atlanta Church presents A Talk by Deepak Chopra, Tonight at 7:30." Universal energies focused their time and space perfection on me right then and there. I heard a voice in my head say... "Turn here now" … and I did. And so began "Jay's Most Excellent Adventure into Spiritual Living!"

As I walked toward the Church, I beheld lots of excited folks milling about in a happy way. Smiles, hugs and laughter were beheld and heard, and I thought, "This looks good!" As I stepped into the beautiful foyer, I was welcomed by a lovely lady who asked me if I would like to join her and her friends.

"Absolutely," I happily replied and right away made my first of many friends at Unity. I kept hearing the word "Namaste" and asked what the word meant. Hearing "the Divine in me beholds the Divine in you" certainly gave a one-word explanation to the source of the happy and loving vibe that filled the room...as well as me!

That next Sunday, I decided to check out the 11:15 service. I witnessed all things new (to me) with beautiful music, a wonderfully inspired talk and lots of singing, hand holding and hugging! A most interesting turn of events, I thought.

Ten years down the road, with full life living and growth both personally and in church community, it still continues! And it is very Good!

A year or so passed after that first grateful step into Unity, when I was asked by a choir member to come "and join in the fun!" I thought, does this spokesperson for the universe, extending a loving invitation, understand that the last time I sang in a choir was back in Jr. High School 50 some years ago?

"There's no try out," he said. "Just show up and you're in."

Once again, I listened to my still small voice telling me to say "yes." And sing I did. I made new friends and got to enjoy Rev. Richard's masterful teaching. I experienced gifting the congregation with music! Many wonderful memories were made but the most vivid is the first time we sang "God Is" at a memorial service. I was in tears by the second verse, it was so powerful. I'll never forget that "full contact" emotional feeling. Thank you God for that experience and so much more!

Because I have been a photographer since I was a kid,

I'm usually always packing a camera with me so that I'm always ready to take that "interesting" shot. So while singing with the choir and admiring the view of the church and congregation from the platform, I envisioned taking a picture looking out into the congregation so that they could see what we could see. I followed the vision to fruition by taking various shots at different services. I was amazed and quite happy with the results! Some of these pictures have been used in the UNAC web site, which makes me feel honored and proud. My all-time favorite Unity picture, though, is the one taken from the platform at the Christmas Eve Candle Lighting service of 2011. To me, it captured "spiritual time and place perfection."

Along this same time, I was invited to be a part of a new men's group, which became The Men of Unity. We adopted a mission statement: to implement a spiritual vision that includes, unites, and serves. Along the way, Andrew Bonar, the leader of the group for its first year or so was moving back to Scotland, and he put out a statement that a new leader would need to step forward in order for the group to continue. A month-long silence ensued with nary a peep from the members. I personally could not accept the fact that a "fade out" would be our fate. Once again the universe came "a calling!" With much trepidation, I answered the call and said "Yes" to the role of leader of The Men of Unity. Turns out, I had leadership skills that were just waiting to emerge. Turns out, that if you show up consistently and authentically, good things happen!

My journey with my brothers in The Men of Unity has been amazing. I have experienced wonderful growth, friendships and success as we continue to provide both behind the scenes and front line service to our church. We have a second Saturday breakfast meeting that feeds us both spiritually and physically, and it is Very Good! The Men of Unity is a strong and vital ministry within our church and I am proud to be part of it. I'm so glad I was "playing attention" and was willing to answer the call to service.

My travels within the church community also included a two-year stint as a Unity Prayer Chaplain. The wonderful training taught me to how to actively listen and to pray affirmatively with an open and loving heart and offered me a way to serve and to hold sacred space. Once again, a "yes" answer to a request from the universe to grow and actively participate was the way! And again, it was demonstrated that a loving and supportive God was my source.

My final, giant, universal, billboard-sized "sign" came three years ago when a calling went out to the congregation that a co-leader was needed to join Debbie Raduka in the Organic Garden. At the time, I was a frustrated ex-gardener with "no row to hoe." The universe knew of my longing to get back to the beauty of gardening and sent me the answer! Once again, I was "playing attention" and I said "yes" to the calling.

My life was further blessed with both new friends and a full time spiritual and physical connection to Mother Earth.

There you have it. I consider myself "all in" and I'm loving it! I'm locked in to the channel of WELOVE, which broadcasts to you 24/7 with universal power from your friends at the Station UNAC, the Church on the Hill. For you "listeners" out there, tune in and "play attention!" More importantly, stop in and say YES. You too will soon see and behold in your heart the vision of Unity North as a glowing beacon of love, faith, joy and community. I know I have! And it is all Very Good. Thank you, God!

How do I catch the wind?

Dr. Eugie Tindal-Kirkpatrick

How do I catch the wind?

It blows in every direction

It's sometimes fierce, and sometimes strong,

sometimes gentle, sometimes calm

It's uncontrollable, uncatchable,

out of reach, beyond earth's grasp

It's a thing of beauty, a thing of destiny!

Where does it come from?

What's its course?

How do I grasp it?

Somewhere, deep inside, I know!

I am the Wind

I am fierce and I am strong,

sometimes gentle, and sometimes calm

I am uncontrollable, uncatchable

A thing of beauty, a thing of destiny!

I AM THE WIND!

A New Beginning

Joanne Perry

I have the Honor and the Privilege to tell you how my life has changed since becoming a member at Unity North Atlanta and living the principles that we teach: knowing and understanding how the Divine nature of God absolutely gives us everything we may want or need if only we TRUST and have FAITH. If you can do that and come from a heart-centered place, know it and feel it deeply, you will be abundantly blessed in all areas of your life.

I read *The Secret*, and I knew about positive thinking. I had million dollar bills plastered all over my house. I had pictures of nice cars, big houses, fabulous vacation spots but none of that ever came true for me because honestly, I did not really understand the key concept of how this worked.

My very good friend, Anne Tyler, asked me if I would like to come and visit her church. At first I thought, oh gosh, not another church. I had jumped around for years searching for that special church that would help me feel complete. I decided to come and visit Unity North, and I knew as I listened to Reverend Richard present his talk, that I was finally home.

But that was just the beginning. I did not know many people in the church at that time, and believe it or not, I am really a shy person. I thought the best way to meet others and feel a part of this community was to get involved. So that is what I did.

The first class I took was the Prosperity Plus class by Linda Minnick. It was in that class I learned about giving freely of our Time, Talents and Treasures. But when the conversation turned to tithing, it was apparent many of us were not prepared for this. Those old paradigms came creeping back in about having to give money, until we really listened to why this was a critical learning concept.

Linda helped us understand how the Universe and God's divine abundance truly works. She asked us to commit for just 12 weeks, whatever we could of our Time, Talents and Treasures. But whatever we committed to in each area, we were to do it from the heart. We were to trust that there is abundance in all areas and see what happened.

I took a leap of faith because I knew there was something better out there for my life. I committed to not only getting involved with my new church by first, and most importantly, becoming a MEMBER of Unity North Atlanta in March of last year, but also by becoming an Usher, joining the Interfaith Ministry, the Hospice Ministry, the Travel Ministry, as well as volunteering to spend the night with our Family Promise families. I also took a very scary leap of faith and committed to 10% of any and all Treasures, including those that would be coming my way in the next 12 weeks!

And oh my, the Treasures showed up in miraculous ways during the next 12 weeks: a tax return refund that showed up two years late, receiving my current year's tax return refund, winning the coverall jackpot at Bingo, receiving a bonus and raise at work, just to name a few. And I always gave the 10% I committed to as a sign of how grateful and thankful I was for this abundance in my life. It seemed the more I gave from my heart and with trust and faith, the more that came to me. Each time that happened, it deepened my belief and trust that God truly does give us what we need and that we live in a world of abundance!

I finally understood how generosity truly worked: believing in my heart, having faith, and trusting that God would provide for me. Not only was there financial abundance, but the more involved I became with my new friends at Unity North, the more joy, happiness, and prosperity came into my life. I am finally at peace now; I am no longer searching for that which will make me happy, for I had it all along, right inside of my heart. I just needed to learn how to trust, have faith, and believe but most importantly, how to give generously of myself and my gifts of Time, Talent, and Treasure to others.

Remember, as Reverend Richard has said many times, Giving is Receiving! You will never live in a world of lack if you give generously from your heart. For me, it was a life changing concept!

I love you guys.

One-ness

Frank Birdsong

From the fiery furnace of the stars we were born, and flung by God's Breath to fill every corner of the vast Universe. There, the Stardust that we once were, cooled and condensed to form all the things of creation that we know and love; the song of a bird on a warm, Spring day, the plaintive cry of a wolf hurled against a cold, Arctic night, and the smile of a baby snuggled safe and secure in its mother's arms.

Although we each are separate and unique expressions of the Creator, we know that we are all connected through the matrix of the energy that surrounds and enfolds us, and, like the glittering dewdrops that are connected by the silky web of a small, grey spider busily spinning in the early morning sunlight, we are formed, then torn apart by the wind, then formed again. We exist…. then we do not. We are…. and then we are not. But always we are connected by the web of Love that flows in, around, and through us and is the source of All Things. And we are fused, eternally and inseparably …..into One-ness. A One-ness that states elegantly and simply…. God Is… I Am… You Are… We Are…. We All are One.

UNA & Me
Debbie House

Unity North Atlanta has been transformational for me. There is warmth, unconditional love, and acceptance that is so welcoming. I experience this just from walking through the doors and finding a seat on Sunday mornings.

Having come as a seeker from a very uncomfortable, fundamentalist background, I was searching for something to fill a hole in my heart.

At first, I didn't recognize UNA as exciting, dynamic, and supernatural as I now do. I was only an observer and not yet a member. My initial thoughts were these people must be a little crazy. *Don't they know they should be worried to death about the condition of our world right now? Don't they have problems? They should be way more solemn and instead they are smiling, singing, clapping their hands, and hugging each other. Some of them are even dancing. Look at these hippies! Good Night, People! We are at church!*

I loved the messages each Sunday and I kept coming, listening, and watching. I discovered and understood that it was what they knew that I didn't that makes the world go around in love, oneness, peace, and goodness. This was an amazing new awareness of the good in the world for me. The coolness factor of these people was off the charts.

Learning the Five Principles answered many of the most baffling questions I had struggled with all my life. It was like finding a huge piece of the puzzle for me. Unity teachings feel so right and resonated with me. Many paths, one God. How amazing was that! *This is it. I'm never leaving.*

In the past, at another church, I suggested an outreach mission for animals. I was gently poo-pooed and re-directed. UNA already had an animal ministry in place! When I saw that, tears of joy popped out and I was so happy and so impressed!

The opportunities for growth at UNA are nothing short of fabulous. We have wonderful spiritual leaders, great classes, awesome music & internationally known speakers visit us every year! I am so blessed to have walked through the doors of UNA.

I am no longer holey, but a little holy and live more wholly.

The Gift Only You Can Bring

Patrice Scattergood

The race goes not to the young and strong
But to those who persevere,
Who hold on tight to their vision
Through the forest of the years.

For all of us have our talents
And to use them you must be brave.
You must have the courage to let your light shine,
Not hide it away in a cave.

For Life is a banquet table
Set for dreamers, poets and fools,
Who care not at all for the status quo
Or for playing by the rules.

If your dream is to build castles—
Or to paint or to dance or to sing—
Come joyfully to the table!
Bring the gift only you can bring.

Two Steps Forward, One Step Back for Me
Drea Nedelsky

When I heard about Unity North Atlanta, I wasn't
looking for a church. I had left the church life well over 40
years earlier when the private Bible college I was attending
decided to make us sign anti-homosexual documents. I realized
that the guilt approach to being saved just didn't resonate in my
life. Being a lesbian pushed me further away from religious
groups because of their narrow views and their intolerance of
diversity. I heard a lot of lip service about how much they loved
you (except when your lifestyle didn't fit their narrow definition
of Christian salvation). Okay, I was bitter. I had hoped to be a
teacher of Biblical history, but faced with prejudice against my
lifestyle, I left the Christian world behind, hurt by the exclusion
and never willing to look back.

Fast forward to 2004. My partner, Maryann, (now 30
years together), was searching for more spirituality in her life.
When I was away on business trips, she attended Unity North.
Knowing that I was a hostile anti-religious person, she waited
until the right time to say she'd been going to this church and
informed me that the minister is a woman, (a rarity in my past

experience) and they were not into being born again or guilt

stories or or or...Okay. She had convinced me to attend. I did

it for her, not believing that I would care.

What a nice surprise and gift I received by attending

Unity North. Rev. Carole was speaking, not preaching, but

speaking from her heart. I was caught up by her passion about

her truths. After that first talk, I felt myself for the first time in

a long time breathe a breath from my missing spirit that had in

fact been buried away so long ago.

I wasn't into the hugging or the hand holding or

singing. I didn't want to be tricked into a false caring group. It

would take a while before I dared to trust that these people at

Unity North could be for real. I can't say it happened over

night, but I allowed myself to stretch and over time the space

felt good. A few times I left during the service, when there were

a little too many "amens" and backslapping that reminded me

of my past.

Early on what encouraged me to return was the

heartfelt sharing and caring part of the service. I didn't feel like

I was in a large church with people trying to show how

important they were, but a one-on-one connection of kind

words was being made. Even though it would only be a few

people that would ask for prayer or share a success of their

prayers, I could hear the silence in the room as those of us

around listened, which felt like a hug of hundreds of people
showing up as one.

One God or Goddess, many path ways, all are
welcomed. "I am the Christ" is what I was experiencing, not a
focus toward a man in a picture, an external being to worship.
We are the Christ that makes us united. People at Unity North
Atlanta began to become real participants in a spiritual
experience of my life

We've been attending now over 10 years. I've watched
the change of ministers, the politics of the board, holding my
breath that spiritual values could slip away and special interests
rule. I still haven't become a member. That door of trust still
hasn't opened for me. I have allowed myself the gift of true
friendships to be formed within the walls of Unity North. I
have attended a conscious living circle, helped at kids' church
camp and numerous special events, volunteered for holiday
projects, garden club, put on the *Red Tent* program to help raise
funds, and encouraged others to attend Unity North.

I think maybe at this point in my life it has become
easier to call this community home ... and in the present
moment, it is good.

Reliquary

Michael Burke

Sunshine scattered through the lazy afternoon

It was the 5th Sunday in the 5th month of 2011

Energies were syncing

Spirits were raising

Before this day had wandered out of night

The Moon had reached its apogee

The place where it is furthest from the Earth

It was also neither waxing nor waning

It was at that millisecond

That twinkling of an I

From one to the other

When emptying becomes filling

When releasing becomes accepting

When letting go becomes letting in

It was transition

True transition

From one to the other

Yet, always in tune

I had no idea how personal

The Moon had been with me earlier

For I was about to transition

Through the power of sound

There are fortunes that find us
When we listen with our souls
My path had brought me a session
With a Shamanic Healer
And as I laid upon the table
And gently closed my eyes
I was re-born
No, un-born
A primal Soul
I became the Heart at the Center of Aum
The Center that has no Center
The Sound that made Sound
The Vibration of Love
The Way God speaks to God
She made sounds that I'd never heard before
At least none I'd heard for the last 7 lifetimes or so
Sounds of impossible origins, but familiar places
Sounds that painted caves...long before we did
Sounds that danced the sky and rippled the water
Sounds that were beyond within and above without
Sounds that were laid as fine as mist upon me
And as deep as roots into me
As if I were an altar

A reliquary

I was the bush not consumed by the flame

I felt feathers where there once were thorns

I felt flight was possible

Not only possible, it was happening

She caressed me in tongues that knew no words

For that is how the Soul hears

And I heard Truth

This empowered my wings to expand

And beat with the rhythm of All that is One

For a while I could fly

Like a wave of sound

And then I became the sky

The sounds that chose to come through her

Were the resonance of the Ancients

The Keepers that disappear

If we listen too hard

They are only seen in absence

And only felt in passing

They have the presence of an echo

When you don't hear the initial sound

They are Channeled Vibration of Source

The tune in the tuning forks

Nature expressed in audible silence

As tones and waves within us

She channeled in vibration and color

A myriad of tones that all came from The One

I was saturated in a bath of Spirit

I was in love

I was Love

I was the Sound that formed Sound

The Sound of the Light

I saw what I was hearing

Like I was hearing with my eyes

And I was feeling with my ears

As if they could touch the vibration

I could feel the temperature

And sense the texture

Of each and every ripple

From each and every wave

It was sanctity awakening

And it swallowed my absolvement

She had opened a portal

That stirred digestion of the Truth within me

My 3rd chakra rumbled in its yellow light

Then exploded into a green star

That spread me like space

Like space on fire

Sparkling and blazing in my rainbow of changes

A Cosmic Chameleon

Completely and Eternally alive in The Sound

In The Word

I am this perpetual resonation

I am the Sound before the Sound

I am the True Reliquary

For I am a Home to God's Breath

And I am a House for Her Glory.

Coming Home
RoseMarie Pacella

My spiritual path began when I was 17 years old. I was raised Catholic and even thought of becoming a nun at one time.

But I felt something was missing; I knew there was more. My family did not understand. They never questioned their religious beliefs. I eventually stopped attending church; it just felt so empty to me. I would wonder, *what are they all getting out of this that I'm not?* I used to question original sin. The idea that I was a sinner because I was born did not resonate with me.

When I went to confession, I would think, *well if I tell them I have not done anything wrong, they will think I am lying.* So I would make up something that I supposedly did to placate the priest, which *was* a lie. I never understood how the priest, a person, could forgive sins. Why did I need someone to speak on my behalf? Were they more special than I was in God's eyes?

I felt that mainstream religion was based in fear dogmas, living for the day you would die.

I just could not buy that my friends who belonged to another religion who were not "saved" were not going to heaven. I could not believe that when a child died, he/she could never see God because he/she had not been christened before they passed.

I began a ten-year search, visiting and practicing many mainstream religions. I even studied with Jehovah Witnesses. I actually had a Baptist Preacher and a Jehovah Witness in my living room at the same time; each one pointed his finger at the other, claiming the other was of the devil. I was told that my family and I were "dead to God" because I was not saved. What was I supposed to be saved from? How was I lost? I opened the door and escorted them out, telling them that I didn't see God that way.

I was also baptized in a Baptist Church, attended Pentecostal churches and non-denominational churches. The latter church was actually almost close to what I was looking for, but not quite.

I started searching in my heart and found I knew who I was, and my truth started revealing itself to me. Each day it grew stronger in me. I realized that religion was man-made, but God Spirit was not. I now know that I am whole and connected and can't ever be lost. It was as if a veil had been lifted.

I knew who I was, where I came from; I could see and feel the connection with all things. I started meditating, something I had never done, and realized that my family and friends already were where they needed to be for their journey of spiritual growth.

Although I was happy and finally secure in my beliefs, I felt alone, like I was the only one who saw this. When I spoke to people about it, they would think I was a little strange. I was even told once, "you know for someone who is not a Christian, you are nice person."

Then as I was going through some personal trials in my life, a very dark time for me, a friend I had met through my children's friends, called me one Sunday to say, "Get your lazy ass out of bed. You are going to church." I asked her what kind of church it was. She said it was sort of a hippie church. Reluctantly, I went with her to attend a service at Unity North.

Not knowing what to expect, I was amazed. I found a lot of people who thought and felt just like me. The excitement I felt that day ten years ago has not ebbed but grown stronger. I am so grateful for my friend, Julie, bringing me to Unity North that day. Since then I brought my significant other, Michael, and told other people about Unity, people who were also searching. Since finding Unity, I have grown and learned more than I ever imagined possible, about how much we are co-creators and how powerful our thoughts truly are, how we are not separate as that is just the illusion.

I see the good in everyone or everything, but also now know even when I may not like someone's actions, the goodness is still there. I have come home, but it is only the beginning of my spiritual journey.

Sanctuary

Laura Hoefener

When I sing
"I am so blessed,"
I turn my gaze up
to windows that open to oceans of blue.
I close my eyes.

I see
the path through the trees which led me here
I remember once a dark night
when I tripped over roots
hidden in the ground,
my feet sinking in mud,
rain soaking my hair.

Today I stand and I sing,
"I am so blessed'.
Looking up through panes of clear glass,
I see light through bare branches
Of the trees that still stand,
their roots deeper now.

Tomorrow it may rain.

The sky will turn gray.

My path will become a stream, then a river,

yet I will stand amongst the rushing waters,

roots growing strong beneath my feet.

My branches spreading ever outwards,

I will turn my face to the sky,

and through those wide windows,

I will see light.

Acknowledgements

There are a number of people who made this book possible, and I would like to take a moment to express my gratitude.

Thank you to Reverend Richard Burdick for leading a spiritual community that has given all of us a place to call "home." You inspire all of us to live the Unity principles and to learn from our experiences, and you motivate all of us to be better people. Thank you to Diane Glynn for all of the work you do to ensure that our home continues to thrive. Thank you to both of you for giving me the opportunity to put this collection together and to share it with the world.

Thank you to Reverend Carole O'Connell and the founders of Unity North Atlanta Church. We are forever grateful to you for creating such a wonderful spiritual community and giving us all the opportunity to become a part of it.

Thank you to Gail Hogue for the beautiful photograph that is featured on the cover of this collection, and thank you Lester Herbertson for your lovely cover design.

Thank you to Kim Grayson for proofreading this collection and giving us another set of eyes to ensure everything was in its right place.

ACKNOWLEDGEMENTS

Thank you to my parents. Without your love and support, I would not be able to do any of the things that I love. Many parents would not be too thrilled at the prospect of their child announcing she is going to be an English major, sing songs, and write books, but you have always supported me. I would not be able to live by the Unity principles and pursue my passion without all of the encouragement and opportunities you have given me.

Thank you to Kayesha Belnap for introducing me to Unity North Atlanta Church back in 2003. You have been an integral part of my coming of age, and you changed my life in so many ways.

Thank you to Julie Boniger for your passion for this church as you encourage everyone to share their creativity and shine their lights with the UNAC community. Thank you for your friendship, g-chat advice, and strawberry margaritas.

Thank you to David Smith for all of your love and support, for encouraging me to pursue projects like these, and for inspiring me to always speak my truth. Thank you for being a loose cannon; it's one of the things that I love about you.

Thank you to all of the wonderful contributors for sharing your poems and your stories. Thank you for letting us see how UNAC has changed and shaped your lives. I greatly appreciate the beautiful and unique ways each and every one of you expresses your creativity.

Thank you to all of the staff, board members, members, and congregants of UNAC for everything you do to create such a thriving spiritual community, such a dynamic family. Thank you for giving each of us a place where we can support each other and help each other grow.

Last but not least, thank you, dear reader, for reading this collection. We hope that you have been inspired and uplifted by our stories and poems. Love to all of you.

Sara Crawford

43251707R10094

Made in the USA
Charleston, SC
22 June 2015